Getz/Gilberto

33 1/3 Global

33 1/3 Global, a series related to but independent from **33 1/3**, takes the format of the original series of short, music-based books and brings the focus to music throughout the world. With initial volumes focusing on Japanese, Brazilian, and European music, the series will also include volumes on the popular music of Australia/Oceania, Africa, the Middle East, and more.

33 1/3 Japan

Series Editor: Noriko Manabe

Spanning a range of artists and genres—from the 1960s rock of Happy End to technopop band Yellow Magic Orchestra, the Shibuya-kei of Cornelius, classic anime series *Cowboy Bebop*, J-Pop/EDM hybrid Perfume, and vocaloid star Hatsune Miku—**33 1/3 Japan** is a series devoted to in-depth examination of Japanese albums of the twentieth and twenty-first centuries.

Books in the Series

Supercell's *Supercell* featuring Hatsune Miku by Keisuke Yamada
Yoko Kanno's *Cowboy Bebop* Soundtrack by Rose Bridges
Perfume's *GAME* by Patrick St. Michel

33 1/3 Brazil

Series Editor: Jason Stanyek

Covering the genres of samba, tropicália, rock, hip hop, forró, bossa nova, heavy metal and funk, among others, **33 1/3 Brazil** is a series devoted to in-depth examination of the most important Brazilian albums of the twentieth and twenty-first centuries.

Books in the Series

Caetano Veloso's *A Foreign Sound* by Barbara Browning
João Gilberto and Stan Getz's *Getz/Gilberto* by Bryan McCann
Tim Maia's *Tim Maia Racional* Vols. 1 & 2 by Allen Thayer

Getz/Gilberto

Bryan McCann

BLOOMSBURY ACADEMIC
NEW YORK • LONDON • OXFORD • NEW DELHI • SYDNEY

BLOOMSBURY ACADEMIC
Bloomsbury Publishing Inc
1385 Broadway, New York, NY 10018, USA
50 Bedford Square, London, WC1B 3DP, UK

BLOOMSBURY, BLOOMSBURY ACADEMIC and the Diana logo are
trademarks of Bloomsbury Publishing Plc

First published in the United States of America 2019

For legal purposes the Acknowledgments on p. vii constitute an extension
of this copyright page

A catalog record for this book is available from the Library of Congress.

ISBN: HB: 978-1-5013-2396-6
PB: 978-1-5013-2395-9
ePDF: 978-1-5013-2397-3
eBook: 978-1-5013-2398-0

Series: 33 1/3 Brazil

Typeset by Deanta Global Publishing Services, Chennai, India
Printed and bound in the United States of America

To find out more about our authors and books visit www.bloomsbury.com
and sign up for our newsletters.

Contents

Contents

Acknowledgments

I would like to thank Jason Stanyek, editor of the 33 ⅓ Brazil series, for soliciting this manuscript and encouraging me throughout. Jason's careful comments on my musical analysis were particularly vital. Thanks also to Leah Babb-Rosenfeld, Katherine De Chant, and everyone else at Bloomsbury for their help.

Anthony Deldonna, comrade-in-arms and co-teacher, provided sage advice and a keen critical ear. My thanks to colleagues in the History Department at Georgetown University for creating a vibrant community of historical inquiry, and to those in the Music Department for making a social and cultural historian feel welcome.

Chris Dunn, Charles Perrone, and Edésio Fernandes asked incisive questions and pointed me toward key sources. Tory Broadus, Alyssa Graham, and Doug Graham provided valuable encouragement on the draft. Michael Abate encouraged me to take the project on. I am grateful to the community of scholars of Brazilian music, particularly Ruy Castro, Sérgio Cabral, Jairo Severiano, Carlo Pianta, David Treece, Carlos Sandroni, José Roberto Zan, Andy Connell, Fred Moehn, and Daniela Thompson, for the work that helped guide this inquiry. Long live WPRB-FM, where I heard most of this music for the first time.

I am forever grateful to my family, Helena Moraski, Jay McCann, Sean McCann, and Moira Moderelli, and especially to Mary Hunter, Booker McCann, and Seamus McCann. You make it all meaningful.

1 Introduction

Getz/Gilberto is the album people think of when they think of bossa nova. (People outside of Brazil, at least—Brazilians tend to have a more complicated relationship to the record.) How did it achieve this iconic status? And why did the album—particularly the single "The Girl from Ipanema"—become a global pop smash in 1964 and 1965? The answer to the first question is João Gilberto. The answer to the second is Astrud Gilberto.

João Gilberto, as both singer and guitarist, was the most important figure in creating the sound of bossa nova. *Getz/Gilberto* captured his sound more completely than his previous Brazilian recordings had, and introduced him to a broad, international audience. Gilberto made several other great albums, and his many fans may quibble about which is his best. But there is no question that *Getz/Gilberto* is his best known, the one he is identified with in most of the world.[1]

João Gilberto's importance in creating the definitive sound of bossa nova notwithstanding, it was Astrud Gilberto who made the album a smash hit. A record featuring João Gilberto along with tenor sax player Stan Getz might have climbed the jazz charts on its own. But it was the participation of Astrud that enabled it to cross over to pop success. Astrud provided the ineffable allure that made the album irresistible.

This is unsettling for many bossaphiles. Astrud was by far the least experienced participant at A&R Studios on W 48 St in Manhattan for the recording session, on March 18 and 19, 1963. (The album was not released until March of the following year.) She was twenty-two (b.1940), had been married to João for three years, had sung in public only a few times, and had never made a record. João, born in 1931, had been a star since 1958, when he recorded the 78 rpm single "Chega de Saudade," widely considered the first bossa nova recording. Antonio Carlos Jobim, better known as Tom, composed "Chega de Saudade," along with lyricist Vinicius de Moraes. Jobim was nearly as decisive as Gilberto himself in creating the genre of bossa nova. Jobim played piano on *Getz/Gilberto*, composed six of its eight songs, and served as musical director. At thirty-six (he was born in 1927 and died in 1994), he was an experienced hand in all aspects of the recording industry and had a long string of popular successes in Brazil to his name.

Stan Getz was the best known of the participants in the United States. He had emerged as a soloist in the big bands of the 1940s and gained prominence as a leader in the cool jazz scene of the 1950s. He was only thirty-six (he was born in 1927 and died in 1991), but was already on his second comeback. Producer Creed Taylor had already demonstrated his own keen ear and made a name for himself by founding the cutting-edge Impulse! jazz label in 1960. And he had a recent commercial success under his belt with his production of the 1962 album *Jazz Samba*, featuring Getz and guitarist Charlie Byrd playing bossa nova, backed by a band of US jazz musicians.

The other musicians on *Getz/Gilberto* were little known outside the nightclubs and recording studios of Rio de Janeiro, but were experienced professionals. Milton Banana was one of the drummers who had defined the sound of bossa nova percussion on the drum kit. Sebastião, or Tião, Neto was the go-to bass player on Rio's bossa scene. (As a curiosity, Tommy Williams, who did not play on the session, was credited on the original album, instead of Neto.) Both were known for their unerring, restrained accompaniment.

It was the relatively inexperienced Astrud who caught the public's attention, however, and who made the record instantly recognizable. Listeners all over the United States, and then around much of the world, called their local radio stations to request the record by that Brazilian girl. Not everyone was happy about this. Many established Brazilian musicians never accepted Astrud's success. They portrayed her as lucky rather than talented, in the right place at the right time. They said it could have been any girl from Ipanema in the studio that day. (Astrud Gilberto was originally from Bahia, in Northeastern Brazil, but the hit single marked her as the girl from Ipanema, nonetheless.)

In retrospect, it is clear that Astrud Gilberto's apparent lack of polish contributed to her appeal. She sounds fresh and unrehearsed on the record. She presents a blank canvas for the projection of the listener's fantasies—fantasies about Rio and its sensual delights, and about Astrud herself. Those who resented her success mistook her simplicity for lack of talent. But simplicity *was* her talent. She knew what not to do.

Her simplicity also fed rumors that her participation was accidental, including the legend that João refused to sing the English lyrics for "Girl from Ipanema," forcing the amateur Astrud to step in, and a star was born. This is not exactly true. Taylor may not have had Astrud in his initial plans for the record, but Astrud had been an aspiring singer for several years. She had already performed at celebrated bossa nova concerts in Rio de Janeiro, and she lived with the world's most exacting bossa nova performer. Rehearsing with João Gilberto must have been akin to studying karate with Bruce Lee: perfection expected, not for the faint of heart. If Astrud sounded unrehearsed on the record, that was the sound she wanted, not evidence of lack of prowess. (Though, to be sure, she may have been a bit nervous in a New York recording studio.)

It was Astrud who made the album a chart-topper, and who accounts for its place in the pop memorabilia of the mid-1960s. But Astrud only sang on two of the album's eight songs. She accounts for approximately two-and-a-half minutes of the thirty-three-minute masterpiece. It was the brilliant setting that allowed her to shine, and that made the album an enduring touchstone of Brazilian popular music. Most pop hits fade away quickly and are remembered, if at all, as markers of their moment. Does anyone remember "Rag Doll," by the Four Seasons, which topped the Billboard charts the week "Girl from Ipanema" first reached the top ten?

But you probably remember all the Beatles songs that hit the top ten that year, including "I Want to Hold Your Hand," "She Loves Me," "A Hard Day's Night," and "Love Me Do." And you probably remember "Where Did Our Love Go" by the Supremes and "Dancing in the Streets" by Martha and the Vandellas, hits of that same year. "The Girl from Ipanema" and *Getz/Gilberto* have that kind of endurance. That continuing relevance requires the complete package: great material, great performance and great production. *Getz/Gilberto* has all three, and that is why it remains the iconic bossa nova album.

Again, not all are pleased by this status. *Getz/Gilberto* was not widely celebrated in Brazil. When it came out in March of 1964, it seemed behind the times. It captured a sound typical of the first wave of bossa nova, which lasted in Brazil roughly from 1958 to 1962. By early 1964, Brazil was in full scale political crisis, leading to a right-wing military coup on March 31 of that year. That crisis changed the world of popular music. For those who opposed the military regime—which included the majority of those who made a living in the world of popular music—anyone still singing about girls walking along the beach was seen as having something other than a swimsuit-clad bottom stuck in the sand. As a result, *Getz/Gilberto* attracted relatively little attention in Brazil itself. Jobim's album with Frank Sinatra, recorded three years later, in 1967, was seen as a bigger achievement in Brazil. Recording with Stan Getz, no big deal. Recording with Frank Sinatra: timeless.

For international fans, Brazil's political crisis passed largely unnoticed. It may even have helped that the Rio evoked on the album—sensual, relaxed, a garden of tropical delights—did not match the latest news reports from Brazil. The fantasy of Rio mattered more than the reality. It did not matter to international listeners that this particular version of the fantasy was crafted in A&R recording studios on West 48th Street in Manhattan. (On that note, producer Creed Taylor and recording engineer Phil Ramone, who also owned A&R, deserve much of the credit for the album's warm, crystalline sound.)

At the same time, the fantasy was not a work of sheer invention. It grew out of a remarkably fertile and optimistic, if brief, period in Brazilian history. Bossa Nova Rio existed. In the late 1950s and early 1960s, Rio de Janeiro was a place of endless musical invention and visual delight. It was a place where old social hierarchies seemed to be crumbling, where racial relations seemed not only amicable but generative, where winning the World Cup and making brilliant music was something Brazilians did because they couldn't help themselves. Even at the time, this was partly an illusion. Rio was then, as now, a city of catastrophic inequality and racial injustice. But the musicians who created bossa nova were not wrong in seeing the late 1950s and early 1960s as a moment of cultural invention and real social achievements. Bossa nova grew out of and expressed the aspirations of that brief, golden period.

Understanding *Getz/Gilberto* requires understanding not just what happened in the studio in March 1963 and after release of the record in early 1964. It also requires understanding Bossa Nova Rio and its evanescent promise. To that end, the chapters that follow intersperse close analysis of the music on *Getz/Gilberto*, biographical sketches of the participants, and an investigation of the context in which bossa nova initially emerged. The fantasy version is preserved forever on *Getz/Gilberto*. The real version is even more interesting, if slightly less lovely.

2 What Is Bossa Nova?

Bossa nova is a popular musical genre characterized by samba rhythm, chromatic harmony, moments of apparent dissonance or tension between melody and harmony, softly sung vocals lacking in vibrato, and lyrics in Brazilian Portuguese, often evoking aspects of life in Rio de Janeiro, with particular emphasis on sun, sea, and sand. Not all characteristics need to be present for a song to be considered bossa nova. Two or three in the right proportion will often do. Like any popular musical genre, bossa nova has a strong core and indeterminate boundaries.

Bossa nova can be played with any instrumentation but is typified by arrangements featuring nylon-string acoustic guitar or piano and vocals, often with additional accompaniment. All the material on *Getz/Gilberto* is classic bossa nova, embodying the salient characteristics of rhythm, harmony, melody, vocal style and lyrical subject matter, in typical instrumentation.

Bossa nova is often characterized as a combination of samba and jazz, and this is true, in part. But bossa also draws on other sources for its harmonic inspiration, such as the Impressionist music of Debussy. And not all samba-jazz is bossa nova: various combinations of samba and jazz existed before the emergence of bossa nova. As the term "bossa nova" became common in the early 1960s, it occasionally subsumed some of these preexisting combinations of samba and jazz, such as big-band arrangements of samba standards. But it would be more accurate to say that bossa nova emerged from a period of fruitful experimentation with combinations of samba and jazz in Rio de Janeiro in the late 1950s, and then characterized this experimentation between 1958 and 1964. (From 1964 on, bossa nova splintered into various branches, some of which doubled back on earlier formulations of samba and other Brazilian rhythms, in a loosely defined genre known as Música Popular Brasileira, or MPB.)

Bossa nova started as a style and cohered into a genre. João Gilberto and Tom Jobim originated the style with innovations they made in 1957–58—Gilberto as guitarist and vocalist, Jobim as composer. Their innovations influenced other composers and performers in Rio de Janeiro's music scene. By 1959 there was a growing musical cohort playing in this style. The early cohort included singer Nara Leão, who hosted informal jam sessions in her family's Ipanema living room, as well as composers Carlos Lyra, Ronaldo Bôscoli, and Roberto Menescal. The importance of Newton Mendonça and Vinicius de Moraes as lyricists was also fundamental. As bossa nova's elements became part of a shared musical vocabulary, the style cohered into a genre, characterized not just by a way of playing, but by a body of work and a way of thinking and talking about the music.

That body of work and the way participants thought and talked about it were firmly rooted in the context of late 1950s and early 1960s Rio de Janeiro. It was a period of economic growth and of the expansion of a middle class with new acquisitive appetites and opportunities. Brazil's domestic automobile industry began a long period of rapid growth. Construction of middle-class apartment towers in the beachside neighborhoods of Rio de Janeiro, served by new highways and tunnels, reshaped the city. Brazilian modernist architecture, defined by swooping curves of unadorned, poured concrete, determined the new look of public buildings and captured international attention.

It was also a period of social mobilization and debate about race and inequality. Within Rio de Janeiro, attempts to evict *favela* residents in the mid-1950s provoked backlash and the emergence of a strong favela land rights movement. Cultural groups like the Teatro Experimental Negro (Black Experimental Theater) pushed for openings in the city's insular high-cultural circles. Brazil's government had promoted a semi-official assertion of racial democracy since the late 1930s, denying the existence of racism in Brazil. But in the late 1950s, university scholars began to question this assertion, demonstrating the persistence of racial inequality in a society strongly shaped by the legacy of African slavery. In the countryside, landless farmers pushed for agrarian reform, a mobilization greatly invigorated by the Cuban Revolution of 1959.

Traditional gender relations changed. *Brotinhos*, or sprouts—young women in their late teens—ventured into the streets and onto the beaches of the city without male accompaniment. They engaged with the risks and delights of city life on their own terms. Rio's swimsuit fashions changed in the 1950s to emphasize secondary sexual characteristics: form-fitting maillots with daring décolletage and hip lines for women, tight square-cut shorts for men. (Bikinis did not become common on Rio's beaches until the mid-1960s.) Display of the body and physical manifestations of health, youth, and exuberance were paramount. *Despojado*—relaxed, informal, unpretentious, lacking unnecessary adornment—was the ideal state, in fashion and in social relations more generally. The trendy, upper-middle-class South Zone beach neighborhoods of Ipanema and Leblon were understood to represent the cutting edge of this style.

All of these trends shaped Bossa Nova Rio. And the music reflected each, in different ways. This is a streamlined history of the emergence of bossa nova and its social context. For each of these characteristics and trends there is a complicating factor or relevant nuance to be considered. Regarding the music, specifically, one can point to figures like pianist and composer João Donato, to composer and vocalist Johnny Alf, or to vocalists Dick Farney and Lúcio Alves, all of whom were performing music with some of the key attributes of bossa nova before 1958. Donato, Alf, Farney, and Alves helped set the stage for bossa nova, influencing both the music and the performance style of figures like Jobim and Gilberto. Brazilian guitarist Laurindo Almeida, who had been playing jazz in Los Angeles since 1947, recorded pioneering collaborations with American saxophonist and flutist Bud Shank in 1953. Almeida's work was relatively unknown in Brazil, but later was taken to be a precursor of bossa. Composer Luiz Bonfá forged a path intersecting with those of Jobim and Gilberto. The list could go on. But if bossa nova teaches us anything, it is that simplification can be a virtue. Stripping vibrato from the vocals reveals the subtlety of the harmony more clearly.

And in the stripped-down, *despojado* version of the emergence of bossa nova, it is João Gilberto and Tom Jobim, above all, who defined the genre. This is the essence. Gilberto was a guitarist and singer from Juazeiro, a dusty crossroads city in the interior of the northeastern state of Bahia. Like most talented musicians looking to make a career in the industry, he found his way to Rio de Janeiro, arriving in the capital in 1950. (Rio was the capital until the inauguration of Brasília in 1960.) Gilberto performed in Rio with a vocal quintet known as the Garotos da Lua (Moon Boys) in the early 1950s, singing the kind of melodramatic samba that dominated radio airplay in Rio in that period. His career failed to take off. He fell into depression. He left Rio in 1955 for a gig in the southern city of Porto Alegre, far from the competitive musical industry of Rio. Gilberto spent much of his time in Porto Alegre studying harmony and refining his technique.

Toward the end of 1955, he withdrew even further, relocating temporarily to Diamantina, a remote former diamond mining town in the mountains west of Bahia, where he moved in with his sister. Gilberto spent eight months in Diamantina, much of it in the bathroom of his sister's house, playing guitar and singing to himself. He emerged with his approach to music fundamentally transformed.

Gilberto's new approach to guitar was defined by a pattern he played with his right hand. He played a single bass note with his thumb on the strong beats of every measure (on the one and two of a 2/4 time signature, typically). And he used his index, middle, and third fingers to play three notes of a chord simultaneously, in counter-rhythm to his thumb. Gilberto kept regular, even time with his thumb, the way a musician playing the *surdo*, or bass drum, would do in traditional samba. At the same time, he plucked a syncopated rhythm with the index, middle, and third fingers of his right hand. This pattern was similar to that played on the *tamborim* in traditional samba. The Brazilian *tamborim* is a shallow drum without jangles, played with a stick, producing a sharp, dry report that can be heard above the blend of other percussive sounds. Gilberto distilled samba rhythm by marking the measure with his thumb, playing a typical tamborim pattern with his index, middle, and third fingers, and leaving out everything else.[1]

This was a new approach both to guitar and to samba. Samba guitarists typically played a combination of bass runs, broken chords (one note at a time), and strummed chords. In a typical samba group, a seven-string guitarist played mostly bass runs in even sixteenth-notes, while a six-string guitarist played mostly chords, either strummed or as broken chords. Gilberto, in his new approach, almost never played single notes, other than the evenly spaced bass notes he played with his thumb. And he almost never strummed. His approach was defined by the alternation between the even time of the bass notes played by the thumb and the syncopated, or uneven time, plucked by the index, middle, and third fingers. That rhythm and counter-rhythm give Gilberto's guitar sound its pulsating momentum. This became known as Gilberto's *batida de violão*, his guitar pattern or guitar rhythm. By 1959, it became a decisive ingredient in bossa nova style.[2]

This had the force of revolutionary simplicity. In retrospect it seems surprising no one had tried it before. Gilberto's greatest innovation may have been realizing this approach would take on its true power only by eschewing all other options. For a gifted musician, laying back—deliberately not playing—is harder than playing. Gilberto's new style was defined in part by *not* playing anything but the essential batida.[3]

It bears noting that Gilberto likely did not intentionally reproduce the tamborim pattern with his index, middle, and third fingers. The tamborim pattern is merely one way of describing the pattern. When Gilberto himself was asked to describe what he was doing, he suggested he had been inspired by the rhythm of the washerwomen in Juazeiro as they ambled toward the river with laundry baskets balanced on their heads. The population of Juazeiro was predominantly Afro-Brazilian, and nearly all the washerwomen of that city were Afro-Brazilian. The everyday grace and rhythm of their work and social interaction were shaped by deep currents of the Black Atlantic World. It is worth keeping both these explanations in mind. Thinking about the tamborim pattern reminds us that Gilberto's approach was not only rooted in samba, but it *was* samba, or one way of expressing samba rhythm. Like *tamborim* players, Gilberto slightly altered his pattern when suitable. Thinking about the washerwomen reminds us that samba and bossa nova not only grew out of deep Afro-Brazilian cultural inheritance, but that bossa nova musicians believed in the importance of reflecting on that inheritance and deliberately connected their own innovation to these traditions.

Gilberto also changed his vocal style during his stay in Diamantina. In the early 1950s, he had used the vibrato and projection from the chest typical of strong masculine singers of the period. After several months singing in his sister's bathroom, he emerged with a vocal style that was barely above a whisper. Instead of commanding the listener's attention through projection, Gilberto's new style drew its power from subtle inflections in timbre and rhythmic placement, singing slightly ahead of or behind the beat. It was a style that asked the listener to lean forward. It was also one that depended on nearly ideal conditions of amplification and recording, when performing in a bathroom was not an option.

Gilberto returned to his parents' home in Juazeiro following his sojourn in Diamantina, spending two months there (plenty of time to observe the rhythm of the washerwomen). By early 1957, he made his way back to Rio de Janeiro. Once back in the capital, he sought out Tom Jobim, and demonstrated his new style for the young composer. This was typical of Gilberto. Both before and after his Diamantina sojourn, he was known for his peculiar sense of social graces. He would identify musicians he wanted to play with and would simply show up at their home late one evening, unannounced and without necessarily having met them previously. In this case, Gilberto had known Jobim previously, but not well. Their reacquaintance in 1957 would mark the start of a pivotal collaboration.

Gilberto had good reasons for his choice. Jobim had recently become prominent through his work as composer for *Orfeu da Conceição*, a musical play with book and lyrics by the poet Vinicius de Moraes. (De Moraes, who was born in

1913 and died in 1980, was an elder statesman of the bossa nova crowd.) *Orfeu da Conceição* sets the myth of Orpheus and Eurydice in Conceição, a predominantly Afro-Brazilian hillside neighborhood overlooking downtown Rio de Janeiro. The Valongo, the nefarious slave market of nineteenth-century Rio de Janeiro, lay at the northern end of Conceição. The Valongo was gone by the 1950s but its memory lingered on, as did its legacy among the local population. The city's docks lay only a few blocks away, and many of the residents of Conceição were dockworkers. When de Moraes wrote the original script in 1954, he emphasized the juxtaposition of classical and Afro-Brazilian traditions not only in the setting and plot, but in the language. He then sought out a composer who could accomplish the same in the music.

Jobim was the ideal candidate: he had grown up in Rio and was deeply attuned to its popular sensibilities. But he had also studied harmony with the German composer Hans Joachim Koellreutter, who had fled the Nazi regime for Brazil in 1937. Koellreutter exerted an enormous influence on Brazilian arrangement and composition, familiarizing his students with avant-garde European techniques such as serialism (using all twelve tones of the chromatic scale in determined series as the basis for composition) and atonalism (composing with the chromatic scale in a way that resists a single tonal center or key). Koellreutter encouraged liberal but flexible use of these concepts, emphasizing above all the importance of developing an original approach through synthesis of diverse source material. Jobim's music for *Orfeu da Conceição* did precisely that, drawing on Afro-Brazilian music as well as the

European concert tradition. Jobim's work stood out for its combination of straightforward but haunting melodies and intricate harmony.

Upon their reacquaintance, Gilberto showed Jobim his new style, demonstrating with two compositions of his own, "Bim Bom" and "Hô-Ba-La-Lá." (These two onomatopoetic titles themselves reveal Gilberto's priorities—the sound *was* the meaning.) Jobim in turn played for Gilberto a recent composition entitled "Chega de Saudade" with lyrics by de Moraes.

"Chega de Saudade" is a curious work, drawing on Brazilian *choro* (an instrumental form akin to ragtime), as well as samba and European Impressionism. The composition has a tripartite structure of introduction, part I and part II, with a modulation from minor key to relative major between part I and part II (or between verse and chorus, depending on how one thinks about the piece). This structure derives from *choro*. Rhythmically, however, "Chega de Saudade" is a samba. And its rich harmony includes over forty chords, taking a standard samba practice of altering chords and pushing it beyond traditional boundaries, adding apparently dissonant notes. De Moraes's lyrics for the song turn on the everyday spoken Portuguese of Rio de Janeiro. The title itself is difficult to translate—the English-language version is called "No More Blues," but "Enough of Longing" or "Enough Nostalgia" would be closer to a literal translation. *Chega* in this usage, meaning "enough already", was popular slang. And *saudade* is an Afro-Brazilian term referring to bittersweet longing.

According to Brazilian music historian Sérgio Cabral, Gilberto spent the rest of the night practicing "Chega de Saudade," figuring out how to play Jobim's subtle chord changes in his own guitar pattern.[4] Bossa nova was complete. The term itself, meaning the new wave, or the new thing, would not become common until 1960, and there are various versions for its etymology. But the sound was already fully formed with the meeting of Gilberto and Jobim.

By that time, singer Elizeth Cardoso already had plans to record "Chega de Saudade," and her original recording came out in April 1958. Vocal contingent Os Cariocas recorded a second version of the song, released in July 1958. João Gilberto made the third recording of the composition shortly afterward. This 78 rpm single, with "Chega de Saudade" on side A and Gilberto's "Bim Bom" on side B, came out in August 1958, and is considered the first fully realized recording of bossa nova.

The sound captivated some and repelled others. All agreed it was something new—positively disruptive or maddeningly dissonant, depending on one's perspective. By the time it came out, Gilberto's style had already begun to shape Jobim's new work. Several of Jobim's compositions on *Getz/Gilberto*, particularly "Desafinado," grew directly out of that process, as did the vast and sweeping wave of bossa nova itself. Numerous other composers and performers adopted and adapted the style, adding their own inflections to a sound defined by Jobim, de Moraes, and Gilberto.

The bossa nova wave had crested by 1962 and had already begun to break apart. "The Girl From Ipanema," written in that year, had its own curious origins, the subject of popular lore and extensive debate.

3 "The Girl from Ipanema"

The story goes that one afternoon in mid-1962, Tom Jobim and Vinicius de Moraes were drinking beer at the Bar Veloso on Rua Montenegro in Ipanema when a lovely young woman walked by on her way to the beach. "Olha que coisa, mais cheia de graça" (Look at that, how full of grace), remarked Vinicius. And just like that, the pair was on its way to one of the world's most memorable songs.

The story is plausible. By 1962, Jobim and de Moraes had already collaborated on over a dozen hits, now considered classics of bossa nova. Jobim was the preeminent composer of the genre, and Vinicius his preferred lyricist. Ipanema was where they spent much of their time. It was the neighborhood that exemplified the emergence of Rio de Janeiro's middle class and its lifestyle, one centered around rituals of beach-going and easy sociability. Like most of the bossa nova crowd, Jobim and de Moraes spent much of their time at one of the bars and cafés adjacent to the beach, or in an apartment within a block of the sand. The Bar Veloso was one of those spots. It offered immersion in the sensory delights of Ipanema: a view of the beach, the feel of the ocean breeze, the taste and smell of its salt, the aroma of roast chicken turning on the bar's spit, the sound of cariocas (residents of Rio) calling to one another over occasional car horns, and the vision of beautiful people on their way to and from the sand. Among these was seventeen-year-old Helô Pinheiro, the muse who inspired "A Garota de Ipanema" (The Girl from Ipanema).

Plausible or not, the story is likely not entirely accurate. Jobim and de Moraes were already collaborating on a musical, a follow-up to their 1956 work, *Orfeu da Conceição*. That work not only served a key role in the development of bossa nova, it made Jobim and de Moraes hot properties. In 1959, French director Marcel Camus turned *Orfeu da Conceição* into the film *Orfeu Negro* or Black Orpheus, using original songs by Jobim and de Moraes, as well as by fellow composer Luiz Bonfá (who had played guitar for the original production of *Orfeu da Conceição*). *Black Orpheus* won the Palme d'Or at the 1959 Cannes Film Festival and went on to become a surprise success in the United States. By 1961, de Moraes and Jobim were looking to follow the success of *Orfeu da Conceição* with another stage musical. Early drafts for the new work included a song about a young woman attracting the adoring gazes of the men she passed. Seeing Helô Pinheiro on her way to the beach in 1962 may have done more to help Jobim and de Moraes finish the song than to start it.[1]

But the story is revealing, nonetheless. Jobim and de Moraes were already celebrated figures. De Moraes was a former diplomat, having served for Brazil's Ministry of Foreign Relations in Los Angeles, Paris, and Rome. Even before *Orfeu da Conceição*, he was a well-known poet (a phenomenon that still existed in 1950s Brazil). Jobim, for his part, had already composed nearly a hundred works, including "Chega de Saudade" and "Desafinado." But the pair hung out at an unpretentious bar with sidewalk tables near Ipanema beach. There was nothing unusual about that. It would have been unusual for popular composers to hang out anywhere else, other than the nightclubs of Copacabana. That was Rio: informal, relaxed, *despojado*. There was no ceremony to stand on.

Jobim and de Moraes tried to capture that world in song. That did not mean they limited their focus to middle-class Ipanema. *Orfeu da Conceição* was set among Rio's Afro-Brazilian working class. By 1962, de Moraes was participating in the cultural initiatives of Brazil's left-wing popular front, affiliated with the National Students Union. Jobim was not politically engaged in the same way as de Moraes, but he shared the lyricist's easy familiarity with cariocas of all backgrounds. This familiarity, and de Moraes's political engagement, emerged in many of their collaborations, like their 1963 work "O Morro Não Tem Vez" (The Hill Has No Chance). But the politics in their work was primarily a politics of everyday observation. And in that context, a song about a beautiful young woman walking to the beach and turning the heads of every man she passed by was perfectly suitable.

The new musical they were working on never came to fruition. But they finished "A Garota de Ipanema," with Pinheiro's inspiration. The precise date of completion is unclear, but by August 1962 they were performing the composition in a series of gigs at Au Bon Gourmet, a tiny Copacabana nightclub. Singer Pery Ribeiro released the first recording of the song in March 1963, with a July 1963 release. It was immediately clear that it was pop gold. By the end of that year, several other Brazilian singers had recorded their own renditions. It was no surprise that Jobim and Gilberto had it in their repertoire when they went into the studio with Stan Getz and Creed Taylor in March 1963. US lyricist Norman Gimbel had already written a set of English lyrics for the song, and recording a version of the song with the Gimbel's lyrics was an obvious choice for Taylor.

There are several legends surrounding Astrud Gilberto's participation in the recording, and from this remove it is impossible to determine precisely which of these point to what actually transpired. It is clear that Astrud was not part of initial plans for the recording session and was paid instead for two days work at the daily rate for a session musician. It is equally clear that João Gilberto could not have considered recording the song in English. He was a perfectionist who focused obsessively on pronunciation and intonation, and he barely spoke a word of English. There is no way he would risk it. (Gilberto went on to record in both Spanish and Italian, but these posed comparatively little challenge, as all of the sounds in these Romance languages are included within Brazilian Portuguese. He did eventually record a rendition of the George and Ira Gershwin standard "S'Wonderful," singing the original English lyrics with a charming Brazilian lilt, on his 1976 *Amoroso* album. But he would not have contemplated singing in English in 1964.)

Astrud, in comparison, was the daughter of a German immigrant to Brazil who had married a woman from Bahia (her maiden name was Astrud Weinert). She was born in Bahia, and moved with her family to Copacabana in her youth. Her father taught German, and Astrud grew up hearing multiple languages and spoke English fluently. And she could sing— protestations of jealous rivals notwithstanding. That would have been enough. It did not hurt that she was young and beautiful. Taylor was too savvy to miss a golden opportunity. Astrud, of course, would sing the English version.

It is João who begins, however. He enters singing, playing his trademark guitar batida at the same time. But he is not singing de Moraes's words. Instead, he opens with onomatopoeia: "Jeem doon doon bleem gung gong." Less than three seconds into the recording, we are already fully in the world of João Gilberto. These are sounds that exist in a wordless, imprecise realm, these consonants between *j* and *d*, vowels between *o* and *u*. It is pure Gilbertiana. Listen closely with headphones, and you can hear what Brazilian scholar Carlo Pianta describes as Gilberto's "wet consonants." As Pianta observes, once you hear this detail, you cannot stop hearing it in all of Gilberto's work. He sounds like he has taken a drink of water moments before. This makes rendering Gilberto's onomatopoeia frustrating: it is not quite jeem jung jong, nor is it dim dum dum. It doesn't take long to feel foolish trying to render a nonsense syllable precisely. But for Gilberto, every consonant has a beginning, middle and end, and is to be uttered just so. The glottal *g*'s are deep in the throat, the *j*'s are in the jaw, and everything seems to resonate slightly in the sinus cavity. Described on the page, it sounds more like a visit to the otolaryngologist than a sublime recording. On the recording, it is divine. That is the magic of João Gilberto.[2]

By the time he launches into de Moraes's lyrics, we are hooked. "Olha que coisa mais linda." Gilberto was initially from the interior of Bahia, but his pronunciation here is full of the seductive sibilance of carioca pronunciation, from Rio de Janeiro. (There are several regional accents across Brazil, each with its own characteristics. Rio's accent emphasizes "sh," "ess," "ka," and "tch" sounds, like the soft hiss and clack of a particularly musical radiator.) When he sings the *m*'s in "num doce balanço, caminho do mar," he is almost humming. A slight buzz tickles the eardrum through the headphones.

This is the one facet in which *Getz/Gilberto* indisputably surpassed all prior Gilberto recordings. The sound engineering by Phil Ramone and his assistant Val Valentin is flawless. Back in 1958, Gilberto had shocked producers at Rio's Odeon studios when he requested one microphone for his voice and another for his guitar. Those early recordings, magnificent as they are, do not capture anything like the detail audible on *Getz/Gilberto*. By March 1963, Gilberto knew exactly how to get the sound he wanted, not only out of his voice and guitar, but out of his microphones. Taylor, Ramone, and Valentin were the first to record that faithfully. Or perhaps not so faithfully: their crystalline sound was itself the product of art and artifice, as they mixed a three-track recording into a two-track master and transformed this into vinyl pressings. The sound they produced had a warmth and definition lacking in the prior Odeon recordings. (Some subsequent recordings, such as *João Gilberto en México* of 1970, and the solo voice and guitar album *João Gilberto* of 1973, were equally successful. Live performances were more variable, and Gilberto became notorious for walking offstage when equipment or acoustic conditions failed to meet his exacting standards. To be fair, in the right circumstances, Gilberto was a mesmerizing live performer, and the best recordings of his concerts, such as that of his 1985 concert in Montreux, are stupendous.)

Gilberto sings and plays the first verse alone, and then Tião Neto, Tom Jobim, and Milton Banana enter softly, on bass, piano, and brushes, respectively. Like Gilberto himself, Neto limits his playing to one bass note on the one, another on the two, of the 2/4 time signature, with almost no ornamentation. Neto effectively doubles Gilberto's right-hand thumb, providing a deeper bottom, albeit with more variation in pitch. Banana and Jobim contribute just enough to buoy the rhythm and outline the harmony. Playing samba on drum kit was still a rare skill in the early 1960s, and Banana was one of a handful of innovators in that regard, using subtle variations to incorporate a range of samba percussion lines into his sound.

João plays through the song once, and then Astrud enters. This creates some cognitive dissonance: João Gilberto sings about the girl from Ipanema, but Astrud sings *as* the girl from Ipanema, singing about herself. We can forgive her for putting the observation in the third person, even when it means singing "she looks straight ahead not at he," rather than "she looks straight ahead not at me." Again, legends surround this solecism, including one that Taylor did not notice it until it was too late to change it. This is not persuasive: Taylor had an ear for detail, and neither he nor Ramone could have mistaken "he" for "me." Instead, it seems likely that Taylor recorded it this way because he realized it was charming: along with Astrud's light accent, it reminds us that she is Brazilian, and underlines her apparent naiveté.

Norman Gimbel, on the other hand, deserves less indulgence. As previous critics have pointed out, in the original lyrics, "olha que coisa mais linda, mais cheia de graça" is written in samba rhythm. The *que*, *mais*, and *de* come just before the one and two of the 2/4 time signature. This is samba syncopation in action. "Tall and tan and young and lovely," on the other hand, is perfectly square, rigidly on the beat. Pop perfection overcomes all other concerns, however.

It also bears noting that in his opening statement, syncopation of Brazilian Portuguese notwithstanding, João Gilberto places his key stresses on the beat (*olha*, *coisa*, *linda*, *cheia*). Astrud, in contrast, brings a lilt even to the plainspoken "Tall and tan and young and lovely." The act of translation seems to bring these disparate approaches together, in an alchemical pop synthesis.

Getz, for his part, swings effortlessly. He was as obsessive about his sound as Gilberto, and his solo on "Girl from Ipanema" is mellifluous and rhythmic at the same time. As with Gilberto's approach, Getz's is notable for what it leaves out. He stays close to the melody with little ornamentation. His variations are more rhythmic than melodic. Jobim plays the verse melody, and Astrud returns for the bridge, first verse and coda while Getz riffs in the background to close the recording.

At more than five minutes long, the song was too long for radio airplay. Using the same recording, Taylor cut an edited version, slicing out João's opening vocals after the onomatopoeic intro and moving directly to Astrud. João's legion of worshippers still consider this sacrilege, but it helped make the song a radio hit. The shortened radio version is now known mostly to collectors. It is the album version, with João Gilberto in full glory, that endures.

Figure 1 *Photo: José Medeiros, "O Brotinho Ivanira," 1950s, Rio de Janeiro (Instituto Moreira Salles).*

4 The Siren Song

There is a siren song of Rio de Janeiro: a beautiful woman (or perhaps a beautiful man) will emerge from the waves, walk directly toward you, and fulfill your heart's desires. It is the siren song that continues to lure travelers to Rio each year. Those seduced completely by the song are trapped forever on the beaches of Rio, somewhere between Leme and Leblon, and can never return home again.

It is a song for tourists, but locals have been known to fall under its spell as well. In the 1950s and early 1960s the siren song was usually about *brotinhos*, or little sprouts—the young women who claimed the beach as their own. As journalist Paulo Mendes Campos described it in a 1960 column entitled "Ser Brotinho" (To Be a Little Sprout), "To be a little sprout means wearing no makeup, sometimes it means acting shameless, with your hair tousled as if it were very windy . . . but throwing fire with your eyes. To be a little sprout is to throw fire with your eyes."[1] The *brotinho* was unpretentious, unbound by conventional social restrictions, unafraid to flirt, and also unafraid to chastise. The cult of the *brotinho* was a mid-twentieth-century carioca variation of the eternal cult of youth and beauty.

"The Girl from Ipanema" is a *brotinho* song, one that fits into a broader pattern. De Moraes writes, "Ah, se ela soubesse, que quando ela passa, o mundo sorrindo, se enche de graça, e fica mais lindo, por causa de amor." (Ah, if she only knew, that when she passes, the world, smiling, fills with grace and is prettier, because of love.) This is the *brotinho* cult epitomized. De Moraes was both enraptured by the siren song and one of its most influential purveyors.

The little sprout in the picture is fifteen-year-old Maria Ivanira Bastos, photographed by José Medeiros for a magazine article on the *brotinhos* and their lifestyle. (To *have* a lifestyle rather than a series of obligations was itself a privilege of the emerging middle class.) Like Astrud Gilberto, Bastos was chosen partly by chance—the editors of *Cruzeiro*, at that time Brazil's most popular magazine, met her in the course of writing an article about her older brother, the popular composer Humberto Teixeira. They realized she would be perfect for a photo spread on a day in the life of a typical *brotinho*. Halfway through the session, Bastos took a brief break in order to plunge into the ocean. Medeiros took the photo as she emerged from the sea, unposed and informal.[2] By chance, her left hand hides her face, preserving the mystery. She looks to the side not at me. The image was used as the cover of *As Cariocas* (The Cariocas), a 1960s short-story collection by popular journalist Sérgio Porto.[3] Like Paulo Mendes Campos, José Medeiros, and Vinicius de Moraes, Porto was one of the key articulators of the cult of the *brotinho*. There is a cluster of late 1950s–early 1960s works about little sprouts on the beaches of Rio de Janeiro. "A Garota de Ipanema" would become the most famous, in part because it perfectly fulfills expectations of the celebration of *brotinhos* and their allure.

5 "Doralice"

After "Girl from Ipanema" come the only two songs on the album not composed by Tom Jobim. Both "Doralice" and "Para Machucar Meu Coração" are the work of titans of Brazilian popular song, the former by Dorival Caymmi, the latter by Ari Barroso. Each carries different strains of the DNA of Brazilian popular music. Both were hits in the 1940s, presented in strikingly different form on *Getz/Gilberto*. By including these two classics, Taylor and the musicians not only pay homage to past masters, they also show how bossa reinterprets the canon, bringing new meaning to its works. Bossa nova was both refreshingly new and deeply grounded.

"Doralice" is a Dorival Caymmi composition from 1945, co-written with Antonio Almeida. Caymmi was a bossa precursor. He differed from most of Brazil's prominent composers of the 1940s in his approach to guitar, to harmony, and to lyrics, in ways that helped shape Gilberto's style. Like Gilberto, Caymmi hailed from the northeastern Brazilian state of Bahia, in Caymmi's case from the state's capital, the coastal city of Salvador da Bahia. Salvador is Brazil's most African city, one where Yoruba words remain part of popular dialect and West African dance, music, cuisine, and religion deeply shape everyday life. Caymmi was renowned for bringing that sensibility to Rio de Janeiro's popular music industry in the 1940s.

Caymmi was largely self-taught as a guitarist, developing his own approach. His rhythmic plucked-chord style established a model for Gilberto's famous guitar batida. That same guitar style also influenced Caymmi's unusual harmonies, as his chromatic transitions from one chord to another resulted in harmonies not commonly used in popular music of the 1930s. Bossa nova would build on this harmonic extension (drawing on multiple other erudite and popular influences, as well). In his lyrics, Caymmi emphasized the natural musicality of Salvador's Afro-Brazilian slang. Although samba emerged as a coherent genre in Rio de Janeiro, it did so in part through the cultural work of black women from Bahia who had migrated to Rio de Janeiro. These women hosted the earliest samba jam sessions, contributed the refrains and dance steps they had learned from their own mothers to its emerging mixture, served as the muses for many of its enduring hits, and were officially celebrated in the annual samba school parade. Caymmi's roots in Salvador and his particular approach to samba composition helped bring that deep connection of Salvador and Rio de Janeiro to the surface. "Doralice" is a perfect example—the syncopation of the colloquial lyrics has the sound and rhythm of samba percussion, a rhythmic meaning at least as important as the literal meaning.

Comparing the original 1945 recording by singer Antonio Almeida and the vocal quintet Anjos do Inferno to the *Getz/Gilberto* recording reveals much about the way bossa distilled the lessons of previous Brazilian popular music and took them in new directions. In the original recording, the Anjos do Inferno transpose Caymmi's harmonies to vocal ensemble, and alternate singing the lyrics and onomatopoetic syncopation. The instrumentation is minimal—guitar and *pandeiro* (tambourine), with perhaps one other instrument deep in the mix, with additional light percussion and what sounds like a cornet, used only briefly. The guitar plays in a typical carioca style of bass-note runs. Lead vocalist Antonio Almeida is relaxed, swinging easily behind the beat. The original recording already has much of the combination of ease and sophistication that would define bossa. But it lacks the cool: the Anjos do Inferno, talented as they were, could not transcend their essential nature: they were the kind of vocal ensemble that pops up from behind potted plants in 1940s musical films. In fact, they *were* the vocal ensemble that popped up from behind potted plants in Brazilian musical films of the 1940s. There is a willfully ingratiating character to their delivery.

Everything about Gilberto's delivery, in contrast, seems effortless, from the opening tchim, tchim, tchim, dim tchim tchim, in vocal syllablization of his own guitar part, through the tricky sibilance of the verse and chorus. It sounds easy until you try to sing it yourself. To the offhanded brilliance of the vocal line, add the pulsing syncopation of the guitar batida. It is a small miracle that Gilberto could do both at once and make it sound as simple as asking for the check and stirring your coffee at the same time. (Gilberto was deeply at ease with the composition, having recorded it in 1960 for the album *O Amor, O Sorriso e A Flor* [Love, the Smile and the Kiss], released by Odeon.)

The lyrics of "Doralice" are themselves casual, everyday speech, the unpretentious protestations of someone who has fallen in love despite his best instincts. "Doralice, eu bem que lhe disse, amar é tolice, é bobagem, ilusão, eu prefiro viver tão sozinho, ao som do lamento do meu violão." (Doralice, I really told you, love is foolishness, it's nonsense, illusion. I prefer to live so alone, to the sound of my guitar's lament.) "Doralice, eu bem que lhe disse, olha essa embrulhada em que vou me meter." (Doralice, I really told you, look at this mess I'm going to get myself in.) *Embrulhada*, meaning mess, muddle, confusion, is slang straight from the streets of Salvador. The lyrics are charming and innocuous, and Gilberto conveys them with the easy grace of skipping a stone over the waves. But every vowel is perfectly shaped, each consonant lovingly carved. When the melody drops and Gilberto draws out the second syllable of *amor* in "Agora amor, Doralice meu bem," it anchors a vocal line so buoyant it seems likely to float away.

Getz seems to draw his inspiration directly from Gilberto, with a light, syncopated sax solo. There is a passage at the beginning of Getz's second run through the verse, beginning about the 1:45 mark of the recording, where he plays a series of eight syncopated notes. When *Getz/Gilberto* became a global smash hit, some Brazilian musicians resented its success, and suggested Getz did not really grasp Brazilian rhythm. Those eight notes should be enough to dispel any doubts on that score. (Getz was likely inspired by the flute accompaniment on the original 1960 recording, but chose his passage wisely.) Banana's brushwork provides the perfect complement. Neto limits himself to keeping time and marking the transition from one chord to another. Jobim lays out for most of the recording. Following the sax solo, Gilberto closes with one of his trademark onomatopoeic phrases, windfall fruit of an irrepressible musicality, and Getz delivers a short, sweet coda. Clocking in at slightly more than two-and-a-half minutes, it is the shortest song on the album, light and ethereal as a Fra Angelico cherub.

Figure 2 *Photo: José Medeiros, September 1956. Oscar Niemeyer, Vinicius de Moraes, Lina Bôscoli, and Tom Jobim backstage at the premiere of* Orfeu da Conceição *at the Teatro Municipal, 1956. (Instituto Moreira Salles).*

6 Backstage at *Orfeu da Conceição*

This photograph encapsulates much of the history of modern Brazil. Tracing its various elements reveals the world that shaped bossa nova and the music of *Getz/Gilberto*, specifically. In September 1956, Niemeyer is Brazil's most prominent architect, in the midst of the most prolific and influential stage of his career. Brazilian Juscelino Kubitschek has pledged to build a new national capital, named Brasília, in the high central plains at the center of the country. Niemeyer and Lúcio Costa have designed the city from scratch, with Costa drawing the plan for the city in the shape of a jet plane, and Niemeyer designing the swooping curves of its major public buildings.[1]

Both Costa and Niemeyer are persuaded their plan will resolve the challenges of the city—not Brasília, specifically, but *the city* in the abstract. Its residential superblocks, suspended on *pilotis*, or stilts, over common areas, will offer density without claustrophobia, and avoid residential segregation by class. Its roadways are designed without intersections, and will enable all from cabinet ministers to their cleaning staff to speed from home to work in minutes. The clean lines and sun-splashed spaces of its ministries will elevate the planning of its public servants. The sleek saucer of the Chamber of

Deputies will gather the people's representatives and blend their voices into the unified national chorus. The dome of the Senate will protect the privileged forum of elevated debate. The broad ramps of the congressional and presidential palaces will remind both citizens and their elected officials that the buildings belong to the people and are open to them. When the photo is taken, Brasília is a dusty construction site four years away from inauguration, and it is still possible to hold to these convictions unwaveringly. In the meantime, Niemeyer has found time to design the set for *Orfeu da Conceição*, and is on hand for the premiere. In the photograph, he looks down, as if from an Olympian height. The world will never measure up to his standards.

Vinicius de Moraes, author of the play, is a former consul in Brazil's Ministry of Foreign Relations. He is in the process of going from diplomat and part-time poet to full-time creative force. *Orfeu da Conceição* and *Orfeu Negro*, the film it inspires, will serve as his calling card as a lyricist. Over the next twenty years, de Moraes will collaborate with a dozen or more of Brazil's most talented popular composers and will become one of the twentieth century's most influential lyricists. In de Moraes's *Orfeu*, the title character is an amateur samba musician, and Eurydice is a migrant recently arrived from the rural north. The underworld is a Carnival parade. As in the myth, Orpheus loses her forever, but his music continues to echo on the hillside.

Orfeu da Conceição reflects the preoccupations and aspirations of the Brazil's cultural vanguard. De Moraes wrote the play specifically for performance by the Teatro Experimental do Negro (TEN), or Black Experimental Theater company. Founder Abdias do Nascimento created the TEN a decade earlier to break open the lily-white world of Brazilian theater and to challenge racism in Brazil more generally. Nascimento is one of the most prominent of a generation of black intellectuals trying to hold Brazil to its egalitarian promise. By 1956, any form of racial discrimination is nominally illegal, and Brazil's government espouses racial democracy. But persistent racism belies this rhetoric, and the TEN aims to hold a mirror to Brazilian society, forcing it to reckon with its own hypocrisy.

Orfeu da Conceição is a musical written by a white diplomat/poet. It is not overtly political in a way that will become common in Brazil's theatrical vanguard in the early 1960s. Its themes are love, obsession, and the endurance of the voice of the people in its music. But the play is a tragedy, one that does not conceal the challenges and privations of the hillside neighborhood. (The 1959 film version by French director Marcel Camus, in contrast, will present the favela as a place of sybaritic pleasure.) *Orfeu da Conceição* marks only the second time that black performers take center stage at the august Teatro Municipal. The theater is a subtropical miniature of the Paris Opera, constructed in the early twentieth century. It has long been the redoubt of a cultural elite that looks to Europe for its forms and expressions. *Orfeu da Conceição* prods that cultural elite to make way for a new set of concerns. In the photo, de Moraes's eyes twinkle as he gazes at Lina Bôscoli. He is the charming bad boy of Brazilian literature.

Lina Bôscoli is de Moraes's third wife—the third of nine, as it turns out. He is 43. She is 24. The slash of her painted eyebrow, the cut of her trousers, the plunging neckline of her cashmere sweater reveal that she is bold, modern, unintimidated in the presence of these renowned figures. She is a daughter of the wealthy Bôscoli clan and a granddaughter of Chiquinha Gonzaga, a pathbreaking composer and pianist of the late nineteenth century. Gonzaga was Brazil's first professional woman composer, a woman who left her husband in order to create her own music publishing company and dedicate her talents to her career. Her most famous melodies remain universally known in Brazil, and shaped the emergence of choro, samba, and, by extension, bossa nova. Lina's brother, Ronaldo Bôscoli, will soon become one of the founding members of the bossa nova cohort. Some will attribute the popularization of the term bossa nova to Ronaldo Bôscoli, in his role as concert promoter. Lina, for her part, embodies the confident, candid sensuality of the modern carioca woman that bossa nova composers will celebrate.

Behind de Moraes and Bôscoli is the young composer Tom Jobim. Jobim's "Se Todos Fossem Iguais a Você" (If All Were the Same as You), with lyrics by de Moraes, is the play's most enduring song. It already has the key compositional hallmarks of bossa nova—gentle samba rhythm, subtle harmony, a simple melody that meshes with that harmony in surprising ways, and elegant, and unpretentious lyrics of love and longing. All it lacks to become full-fledged bossa nova is the performance style of João Gilberto. In the photo, Jobim rests his chin on his fist and gazes to his left, as if tuning into a different set of sounds.

Behind Jobim, a poster for the musical and a call sheet tacked on the door situate us backstage for the premiere of *Orfeu*, for Brazilian history, and for the genesis of bossa nova. It is a music that will reinvent and reinvigorate Brazilian institutions. It will reflect the sinuous curves, the ambition and the optimism of Brazilian architectural modernism. Its aspirations of racial inclusion will rest heavily on the reinterpretation of Afro-Brazilian cultural legacies, and will exist in tension with the white, middle-class origins of most of its practitioners. It will celebrate the modern girl and her independent engagement with the city. And it will spring primarily from the collaborations of de Moraes, Jobim, and João Gilberto.

7 "Para Machucar Meu Coração"

"Para Machucar Meu Coração" (To Wound My Heart) is an Ari Barroso composition from the early 1940s. (The first word in the title is often listed as the more informal and phonetic *Pra*, but on *Getz/Gilberto* it is listed as *Para*.) Barroso was one of Brazil's best known and most influential popular composers and was already relatively well known in the United States as the composer of the classic "Aquarela do Brasil." Usually listed in the United States simply as "Brazil," the song was featured prominently in the 1942 Disney film, *Saludos Amigos*, and again in the 1945 Busby Berkeley film *The Gang's All Here*, starring Carmen Miranda. In "Aquarela" and other sambas from the 1930s and 1940s, Barroso sought to elevate samba to an exalted role as the cultural symbol of the Brazilian nation, and to invest it with patriotic zeal. His catchy melodies, inventive structures, and innovative harmonic progressions gave his compositions broad and enduring appeal. Both João Gilberto and Tom Jobim claimed Barroso as a major influence.

"Para Machucar Meu Coração," one of Barroso's better-known compositions, is a melancholy *samba-canção*, or samba-song. Samba-song's blend of down-tempo samba rhythm with the extended melodic lines and narrative lyrics of romantic song was a staple of the golden age of Brazil's radio singers in the late 1930s through the 1950s. The genre's more heartbreaking examples were known as *dor de cotovelo*, or elbow-pain music. These were (and still are) consoling songs for bereft lovers to sing while they prop their elbows on the window-sill, rest their weary heads in their hands and cry (a pose not so different from the one Jobim adopts in the photograph with Oscar Niemeyer and friends).

"Para Machucar Meu Coração" is classic elbow-pain music, with a lyric about the unwelcome wisdom that comes with heartbreak. The tale of woe begins colloquially, "'tá fazendo um ano e meio, amor, que o nosso lar desmoronou." (Been a year and a half, my love, since our home fell apart.) This conversational Brazilian Portuguese, dropping the first syllable of *está*, was itself an innovation in Brazilian popular music of the 1930s and 1940s, heralding the conversational poetry that lyricists like Vinicius de Moraes and Newton Mendonça would later bring to bossa nova. "Meu sabiá, meu violão, e uma cruel desilusão, foi tudo que ficou, ficou, pra machucar meu coração." (My songbird, my guitar, and a cruel disillusionment were all that remained, remained, to wound my heart.) Good grief, in the truest sense of the phrase.

After this anguished verse, the bridge builds to reluctant acceptance of perspective gained through suffering: "Quem sabe não foi bem melhor assim, melhor pra você e melhor pra mim. A vida é uma escola em que a gente precisa aprender a ciência de viver pra não sofrer." (Who knows, maybe it was better this way, better for you and better for me. Life is a school where we must learn the science of living in order not to suffer.)

The song was first recorded in 1943 by Déo, a singer so popular he was known at the time as the Dictator of Hits. (Déo, whose given name was Ferjalla Rizkalla, also happened to be the son of Lebanese immigrants—not unusual in a context in which much of Brazil's most nationalist music was recorded by immigrants and their children.) Déo's delivery emphasized the inherent melodrama of the lyrics. The arrangement of his original recording, full of orchestral flourishes and dramatic brass, did the same. True to his moniker, Déo's recording became a hit, and the composition became a staple for Brazil's radio singers of the 1940s and 1950s. It is a song that all the Brazilians involved with *Getz/Gilberto* would have heard hundreds of times in their youth.

For all these reasons, "Para Machucar Meu Coração" seemed to be the opposite of bossa nova: it was weepy and unguarded where bossa was restrained and cool, apparently stale where bossa was fresh. But like all of Barroso's great compositions, it has a melodic line that unfurls effortlessly. It was ripe for reinvention.

The *Getz/Gilberto* version begins with Jobim playing a series of chromatic notes, then sparse chords, while Gilberto plays a slightly altered version of his signature guitar batida. Neto and Banana accompany unobtrusively, as ever. We are in very different terrain from the big-band sound of the original version. The greater difference is in Gilberto's vocal rendition. Where Déo strained and sobbed, Gilberto nearly whispers. He is not shouting from the balcony but speaking softly to the memory of an old flame. He makes his opening statement plainly. And, in classic Gilberto fashion, he makes it plainly again, with only the subtlest of modulations. When Déo moans that it may have been better for both of us, it sounds like the rueful dismissal of the scorned lover. Gilberto's tone of reluctant but compassionate acceptance keeps heartbreak at greater distance.

After the bridge, Getz returns us to the verse with a tender improvisation, drawing out his notes in a way that allows his timbre to speak for itself. Like Gilberto, he plays in the open spaces of the samba-song, transitioning from the bridge back to the verse with a plunge from Bb to Gb. Jobim bookends the arrangement with a chromatic passage and a simple send off as Gilberto plays an Ebmaj7 in first inversion (G-Bb-D-Eb).

The *Getz/Gilberto* version changed the song. Most subsequent interpreters have followed Gilberto's lead, such as Rosa Passos and Lula Galvão, in their gorgeous 1997 recording. João Gilberto remains a household name around the world. Déo, the deposed dictator, is a footnote, remembered by a dwindling number of Brazilians who were young in the 1940s. Life is a school, and popular music can be a hard discipline. Who knows, maybe it was better this way?

Figure 3 Photo: José Medeiros. Swimming pool of the Copacabana Palace Hotel, with Avenida Atlântica and Copacabana Beach in the background, 1950. (Instituto Moreira Salles.).

8 Woe Unto You, Copacabana

The Copacabana Palace, inaugurated in 1923, was the place for Rio's elite to see and be seen, and to mingle with illustrious travelers. In some ways, the glitzy hotel represented the opposite of bossa nova's *despojado* spirit. But Rio's smart set knew when to opt for glitz, and when to affect nonchalance. Copacabana's *inferninhos* or little hells—crowded, informal nightclubs that served as samba-jazz laboratories in the late 1950s—were within two blocks of the hotel and depended on its clientele. Figures like de Moraes and Lina Bôscoli were as familiar with the swimming pool at the palace as they were with the after-hours jazz of Bottle's Bar, in a nearby alleyway.

Journalist Rubem Braga knew that well. Braga, a celebrated author of *crônicas*, or chronicles, semi-factual newspaper accounts of everyday life in the city, had introduced de Moraes and Bôscoli in 1951, and remained part of their circle through the 1950s. In 1958, the same year that João Gilberto recorded "Chega de Saudade," Braga published his most famous *crônica*, "Ai de ti, Copacabana" (Woe unto you, Copacabana). The *crônica* is a satirical, pseudo-biblical imprecation against heathen Copacabana, warning its louche denizens of the coming tidal wave that will wash away its many sins.[1]

Braga warned, in the voice of the Almighty,

Woe unto you, Copacabana, because they called you the
Princess of the Sea, and garlanded your front with a crown of
lies, and you let out besotted and vain laughter in the bosom
of the night. . . . Your maidens stretch out on the sand and
rub aromatic oils on their bodies to toast their epidermis, and
your young men use their motor-scooters as instruments of
concupiscence. Lament, young men, and beseech, young
ladies, and roll in the ashes, because your days are finished,
and I will destroy you.

Drawing on Copacabana's association with *Iemanjá*, the *orixá*,
or supernatural entity of the sea in the Afro-Brazilian religion of
Candomblé, Braga promised a watery vengeance befitting the
orixá's preeminence. Addressing himself to Oscar Ornstein, the
maître d'hôtel at the Copacabana Palace, Braga commanded,
"And you, Oscar, son of Ornstein, reserve for Iemenjá the most
spacious quarters of your Palace, for there, among the algae,
will she dwell."

Braga knew that Copacabana's pleasures were a fleeting
gift stolen from the gods. They were also, as Braga implied,
ostentatious simply by context: residents in the favela of
Babilônia, who lacked regular access to clean water, electricity,
and sewage services, could just make out the reclining figures
of those lounging poolside at the Copacabana Palace a few
blocks away. "The inhabitants of your hillsides will fall upon
you howling, and the cannons of your own fortress will
turn against your body and thunder, but the salt water will

take millennia to wash away the sins of a single one of your summers." (It bears noting that in his song "O Morro Não Tem Vez"—co-authored with Jobim—de Moraes would also write about the residents of the hillside descending on the city to demand their just due.)

Braga knew whereof he spoke. He was part of the Copacabana scene. They were all having entirely too much fun, he suggested, and someday soon would pay the price. "Ai de ti, Copacabana" remains a vivid portrait of the world that produced bossa nova, one captured in José Medeiros's image of the swimming pool at the Copacabana Palace. The photograph shows the Copacabana Palace and Copacabana beach as they existed in the 1950s. Public works projects of the late 1960s and 1970s more than doubled the width of both Avenida Atlântica and the beach itself. Some say expansion sacrificed the human scale of the neighborhood in the name of speed and efficiency. Others say the romance was long gone, in any case. By that time, Bossa Nova Rio was a memory. Braga's Copacabana was ultimately destroyed not by tidal wave, but by its internal pressures and contradictions.

9 Stan Getz

Stan Getz was the Tom Hanks of saxophonists. He won awards so consistently that his presence on the ballot seemed to save voters the trouble of splitting hairs: just give it to Getz again. Whitney Balliett, the *New Yorker*'s eminent jazz critic, described Getz as "the poll winners' poll winner. He won the *Metronome* poll eleven years in a row and would probably still be winning if the magazine hadn't gone out of business. He won the *Downbeat* readers' poll eleven times and its critics poll six times. He won the *Playboy* poll seven years and is one of *Playboy*'s All Stars' All Stars."[1]

Getz won the *Downbeat* readers' poll for best tenor saxophonist each year from 1950 to 1959. *Downbeat* was the jazz world's flagship magazine, and in the estimation of its readers, Getz was a better tenor saxophonist than Coleman Hawkins, Ben Webster, and Lester Young in the later stages of their careers, John Coltrane, Dexter Gordon, and Sonny Rollins at the beginning of their careers, or Zoot Sims and Al Cohn at the peak of their careers. Getz was considered unsurpassable.

For some critics, consistent acclaim was in itself dubious. Balliett noted that Lester Young, widely considered the inspiration for Getz's gentle, lyrical timbre, only won two readers' polls in his lifetime. The implication was that true geniuses felt the pushback against their innovations and the popularizers later reaped the rewards. But Getz was more than a popularizer of Young's sound: he had his own genius. In contrast to most of the great jazz tenor saxophonists of the mid-twentieth century, who based their improvisation on the blues, Getz drew more deeply on the American popular songbook. His famous solo on the Woody Herman big band's 1948 recording of "Early Autumn" revealed his gift: he improvised a melody more memorable than the Ralph Burns composition itself, one as graceful and haunting as a Hoagy Carmichael standard.

Getz's long run at the top of the *Downbeat* readers' poll coincided with his evolution from gifted sideman with the Herman band to a leader of small combos throughout the 1950s. He recorded some seventeen albums as a leader or co-leader in that decade. A few of these records featured equally prominent musicians like Dizzy Gillespie, Lionel Hampton, Oscar Peterson, and Gerry Mulligan, but most were made with lesser known personnel, where the spotlight was overwhelmingly on Getz and his ethereal sound.

Throughout most of this decade of acclaim, Getz's personal life was a shambles. He spent the greater part of the 1950s strung out on heroin and barbiturates or struggling through various unsuccessful attempts at recovery, including a six-month sentence for heroin possession, served in the Los Angeles City jail in 1954. His first marriage fell apart soon after, in part because of the heroin, in part because he had fallen in love with Monica Silfverskiöld, a Georgetown undergrad Getz met following a 1955 gig in Washington D.C. Getz divorced his first wife in 1956, and married Silfverskiöld soon after. She was the daughter of a prominent Swedish Olympian and physician, and the couple spent most of the late 1950s in Scandinavia. Getz recorded some of his best work of the 1950s in Copenhagen. Monica Silfverskiöld Getz would later play a crucial role in the recording of *Getz/Gilberto*. When Gilberto retreated to his hotel room, miffed at some perceived slight, it was Monica who persuaded him to make the short trip to the recording studio for the historic sessions.[2]

Getz finally lost his spot at the top of the *Downbeat* readers' poll in 1960, with Coltrane claiming the honor for the first time. Coltrane's heavyweight tenor sound of muscular runs set the tone for a new generation of tenor sax players. The tender lyricism of Getz's 1950s work sounded dated. His hard living, his emotional and physical remoteness and his habit of alienating former friends and bandmates, all seemed to have caught up with him. The 1962 *Jazz Samba* record with Charlie Byrd, followed by *Getz/Gilberto*, and a subsequent tour with Astrud Gilberto marked not just a comeback but an evolution, propelling Getz into a new and substantially different stage of development. Coltrane's emergence notwithstanding, Getz reclaimed his *Downbeat* throne in 1962, following *Jazz Samba*. He went into the recording sessions for *Getz/Gilberto* knowing that bossa nova was both his meal ticket and an opportunity to experiment with an entirely different songbook, one with its own grace and beauty.

It turned out to be one of the most successful of several unexpected departures in Getz's long career. As the child and grandson of Russian/Ukrainian Jewish émigrés, reinvention was part of his family legacy. Getz's grandparents, Haris and

Becky Gayetski, originally left Kiev for London. Al Gayetski, his father, was born in London, and later moved to Philadelphia, where Stanley Gayetski was born in 1927. The Gayetskis moved to New York when Stanley was six. By that time they had Americanized their last name to Getz, the first of several reinventions. Getz grew up in the Bronx, in a neighborhood heavily populated by Russian Jews (the family of his mother, Goldie Yampolski, had also fled the pogroms of Kiev). This was the world later portrayed in E. L. Doctorow's autobiographical novel *World's Fair*, one where parents and grandparents spoke Russian or Yiddish at home and read Tolstoy and the children listened to Benny Goodman and read comic books.[3]

Getz took to jazz easily and enthusiastically. He was already playing professionally by the time he was fourteen. At sixteen, he dropped out of high school and joined trombonist Jack Teagarden's big band on the road. With Teagarden's band, he learned how to survive on the road as a traveling musician. He also learned how to drink heavily, beginning a lifelong substance abuse problem. Over the next seven years, he played with numerous big bands, including stints with Stan Kenton, Benny Goodman, and Tommy Dorsey, before joining the Woody Herman band.

Getz was only thirty-six when *Getz/Gilberto* was recorded, but he already had twenty years of professional music behind him, nearly as many of addiction, and one failed marriage. *Jazz Samba* may have saved his career. *Getz/Gilberto* made him an icon to a younger generation, including listeners who had never heard of *Downbeat* magazine.

Figure 4 *Photography by José Medeiros. Rehearsals for* Orfeu da
Conceição, *1956. (Instituto Moreira Salles).*

10 Bossa, Race, and Politics

In the photo opposite, playwright Vinicius de Moraes reads lines with Daisy Paiva, who plays the role of Eurydice, as the rest of the cast looks on. The photograph reveals the racial aspirations of *Orfeu da Conceição* and also their limitations. Both of these would shape the growth of bossa nova—and subsequent Brazilian popular music.

In his program notes for the play, de Moraes wrote, "This play is, then, an homage from its author and producer . . . to the black population of Brazil, for all it has given to Brazil even in the most precarious conditions of existence."[1] De Moraes recognized the continued existence of racial injustice in Brazil earlier and more deeply than did the vast majority of Brazil's white, middle-class population. Part of his intent in *Orfeu* was to draw attention to that injustice. Inevitably, however, it was de Moraes who was most celebrated. In the photograph, de Moraes holds court, surrounded by a semi-circle of actors from Abdias do Nascimento's Black Experimental Theater group. He is the center of attention, and they are supporting players.

This dynamic shaped bossa nova as well. Bossa nova derived from Afro-Brazilian samba, and several of its most prominent composers and performers sought to pay homage to those origins. But those composers and performers came primarily from white, middle-class backgrounds and continued to move in those circles. Bossa faced a backlash within Brazil, as enthusiasts of traditional *samba de morro*, or favela samba, derided it as the watered-down product of the middle class, corrupted by international influence.

Composer Carlos Lyra pushed for more politicized bossa nova, grappling with racial and economic inequality in Brazil. In 1962, Lyra became a founding member of the Centro Popular de Cultura (Popular Center of Culture), affiliated with the left-wing União Nacional de Estudantes (National Students Union). The *CPC da UNE*, as it was known, advocated revolutionary cultural production, rooted in Brazilian tradition but designed to expose injustice and impel change. Lyra brought de Moraes into the organization, and the two collaborated on *Pobre Menina Rica* (Poor Little Rich Girl), a musical with a cross-class romance and a plot emphasizing the struggle of favela residents against exploitation. Bossa nova singer Nara Leão played the title character—a role that reflected her own background as the daughter of an elite family, increasingly uncomfortable with her privilege.

Over the course of 1963, Lyra and Leão grew more vocal in their dismissal of fellow musicians who failed to demonstrate sufficient commitment to the cause. Leão renounced bossa nova entirely, at least at the rhetorical level. As Brazil hurtled toward political crisis over the first few months of 1964, musicians were expected to make their political affiliations known. Those who demonstrated a commitment to a leftist popular front described the music they made as Música Popular Brasileira, or MPB. It was defined by Brazilian rhythm, acoustic instrumentation, and lyrics depicting social reality, often about class conflict or mobilization. Those who were leery of the leftist popular front tended to gravitate either to lighthearted pop or to rock and roll. (Rock and roll's clear US influence meant it was usually perceived as depoliticized or a product of cultural imperialism, until transformations of the late 1960s made a hash of these categories.) The right-wing coup of March 31, 1964, deepened the split within the world of popular music.

The key figures of bossa nova differed in their approaches to these controversies. De Moraes did not take a political stand as dramatically as did Lyra and Leão, but he became a notable figure of the *esquerda festiva*, or festive left—those adepts of MPB who celebrated their political commitment through music festivals and gala premieres. Jobim took a different path. He embodied a commitment to humanism through conviviality: he was known as a gentle soul, inclined to get along with anyone and leery of partisan affiliation. When asked about his ideology, he described himself as a member of the *direita festiva*, or festive right, but that was primarily a way of brushing off demands for public statements. João Gilberto avoided political controversy by staying out of Brazil for most of the 1960s and 1970s and eschewing interviews.

The mid-1960s political split among Brazilian musicians reflected a broader national divide. One of its perverse implications was to turn attention away from the deeper complexities of race and the popular musical industry in Brazil. The festive left dedicated its attention to resisting the military regime and its general suppression of civil rights. The specific interest in racial inequality that animated *Orfeu da Conceição* was moved to the back burner. The debt that de Moraes referred to in his program notes for *Orfeu* remained unpaid.

11 "Desafinado"

Getz/Gilberto is a masterpiece of an album and contains two individual masterpieces within it: "Desafinado" and "O Grande Amor." None of the other songs on the album rises to their level. "Girl From Ipanema" is a sublime popular hit, but that is a different kind of excellence, one more akin to a bolt of lightning than the Taj Mahal. "Doralice" and "Para Machucar Meu Coração" were both standards of Brazilian popular song before bossa nova, and while the renditions on *Getz/Gilberto* take them in new directions, they cannot break new ground in the way of Jobim's greatest works. "Corcovado" is enchanting, and one of the best-loved tracks on the album—it is Astrud's only song after the album-opening "Girl from Ipanema." But it gets a little tiring after the millionth listen or so. "Só Danço Samba" is a wonderful vehicle for improvisation but does not have the jaw-dropping singularity of the greatest Jobim/ de Moraes compositions. "Vivo Sonhando" is pleasing but I doubt many bossaphiles would put it in the top fifty Jobim compositions. It is "Desafinado" and "O Grande Amor" that repay repeated listening, even after all this time.

"Desafinado" is by far the better known, and the one that has become a jazz standard as well as a bossa nova classic. It was on its way to becoming a standard even before *Getz/ Gilberto,* in both Brazil and the United States. João Gilberto was the first to record the song, on the *Chega de Saudade* album of 1959. The original recording already includes most of the decisive elements of the *Getz/Gilberto* recording, with the exception of Getz. Gilberto's guitar batida drives the recording, and he delivers the lyrics with the same direct intimacy he later brought to the *Getz/Gilberto* version. By 1959, he had already crafted his trademark sound, one he would barely change for the rest of his career. Why mess with perfection?

Aloysio de Oliveira produced the *Chega de Saudade* album. Oliveira was a stalwart of Brazil's music industry—he was a member of Carmen Miranda's backing band in the early 1940s—and was one of the first members of the old guard of Brazilian music to perceive the promise of bossa nova. His production for *Chega de Saudade* rooted bossa nova in the samba tradition while setting its innovations in high relief. The arrangement on the original recording of "Desafinado" included trombone counterpoint and flute accents, elements typical of samba production in the period. It also included a full string section, providing an elegant complement to Gilberto's intimate vocals and guitar.

Gilberto's original recording immediately caught the attention of US-based jazz musicians interested in Latin sounds. Dizzy Gillespie, Laurindo Almeida, and Herb Alpert all recorded renditions of "Desafinado" in 1961 and early 1962, familiarizing jazz audiences with the composition. And Getz and Charlie Byrd had a hit with "Desafinado" in 1962, in a strictly instrumental version. The success of that recording helped pave the way for *Getz/Gilberto*. The rhythm section on the Getz and Byrd recording consisted of Keter Betts on bass, Buddy Deppenschmidt and Bill Reichenbach on drums and percussion, and Charlie's brother Gene Byrd on bass and rhythm guitar—all US jazz players. Their accompaniment is more pan-Latin than Brazilian, drawing on the Afro-Cuban clave that had already become a staple of Latin jazz. Byrd's approach as a guitarist differed radically from that of Gilberto, emphasizing improvised runs on the electric guitar. When Byrd strums, it is mainly to spur Getz on to greater improvisational intensity. And Getz complies—his solos on the 1962 recording are busier and more ostentatious than on the version he recorded for *Getz/Gilberto*. The 1962 performance won Getz a Grammy for best jazz solo.

Creed Taylor produced the Getz and Byrd album, already displaying the affinity for bossa nova he would bring to *Getz/Gilberto*. He recorded the group in All Souls Unitarian Church in Washington D.C., taking advantage of the church's excellent acoustics. It is easy to understand why the Getz and Byrd recording thrilled jazz fans—the composition is a classic, both headliners solo with flair, and the recording pointed toward new horizons for jazz musicians. The 78 rpm single of the Getz and Byrd recording of "Desafinado" sold more than a million copies, unprecedented for a jazz recording.

The rapid proliferation of recordings of "Desafinado" is no accident: along with "Chega de Saudade," it is one of the two canonical compositions that define bossa nova's characteristics. The title itself suggests the first of those characteristics. *Desafinado* means out of tune, in reference to the apparent dissonance of bossa nova—an unusual interplay of melody and harmony that was jarring at first listen, and revealed its

"Desafinado"

compelling subtleties over time. Lyricist Newton Mendonça, in one of his greatest collaborations with Jobim, used this apparent dissonance as his starting point. The song's narrator begins, "Se você disser que eu desafino amor / saiba que isto em mim provoca imensa dor / só privilegiados têm o ouvido igual ao seu / eu possuo apenas o que Deus me deu" (If you tell me I'm out of tune, my love / you must know that causes me immense pain / Only the lucky have an ear like yours / I only have the one that God gave me). (The original composition has an introduction with its own lyrics preceding this verse, but it is rarely performed, and was not included either on João Gilberto's 1959 recording or on *Getz/Gilberto*.) To hear these lyrics sung by Gilberto, owner of an almost supernatural ear for tonal inflection, is to enter into the game of bossa nova: there is more here than meets the ear, at least upon first listen. João Gilberto is out of tune like a fox is crazy.

The next verse offers a quiet manifesto for the genre: "Se você insiste em classificar / meu comportamento de anti-musical / eu mesmo mentindo devo argumentar / que isto é bossa nova, isto é muito natural." (If you insist on classifying my behavior as anti-musical, I must argue, even if I am lying, that this is bossa nova, and it is very natural.) The narrator *was* lying, as it turns out: even for João Gilberto, bossa nova did not come naturally. It took him several months in a bathroom in Diamantina to play like that. But it is definitely musical.

The next verse assures the listener that bossa is not all cool reflection: it has heart. And it also places the genre in the middle-class world of Rio de Janeiro, one of imported luxury goods, where seeing and being seen were of primary importance. "O que você não sabe nem sequer pressente / é que os desafinados também tem um coração / fotografei você na minha Rolleiflex / revelou-se a sua enorme ingratidão" (What you do not know and cannot guess is that the out-of-tune also have a heart. I took a picture of you with my Rolleiflex, and it revealed your enormous ingratitude).

The Rolleiflex is a striking detail in a genre whose lyrics tend to traffic more in eternal substantives like sea, sun, and love than in brand merchandising. Why the reference to precision German manufacturing? Start with the sound of the word: Rolleiflex—or hawllyfleks, in Brazilian phoneticization—is almost unwieldy, but becomes musical in this context, a rocky island in a sea of soft vowels. It is akin to one of Jobim's apparently dissonant notes.

But the narrator also wishes to make it clear that he is not using a flimsy domestic camera—he might be tuneless but he's not cheap. He refers to the Rollei with the same studied informality he might refer to visiting Paris out of season. This shamelessly bourgeois setting annoyed some listeners more than did bossa's apparent dissonance, and contributed to the split in bossa nova ranks that had emerged by the time *Getz/Gilberto* came out. But for Mendonça and Jobim it was honest and candid. They were creatures of middle-class Rio, documenting their world as they created it.

The Rollei reference also formalized what would become a long romance between photography and bossa nova. Jobim's own lyrics for his composition "Fotografia" (Photograph), also from 1959, offer a precise yet tender snapshot of two lovers on a seaside terrace (without mentioning the brand of the camera). Chico Buarque's 1968 lyrics for Jobim's "Retrato em Branco e Preto" (Portrait in Black and White, also known as "Zingaro") play on the idea that both a photograph and a sonnet can offer a portrait in black and white of the artist and his obsessive love. Buarque's lyrics for Jobim's "Anos Dourados" (Golden Years), a 1987 bolero-bossa nova, meditate on the lingering power of a photograph from a love affair that has come to an end. Something about bossa's precise but unsettling harmonies seemed to call out for invocation of the power of photography to make the familiar strange. (It did not hurt that bossa emerged among the eminently photographable golden youth of Rio de Janeiro.)

Meanwhile, the narrator of "Desafinado" continues his protestations: "Só não poderá falar assim do meu amor / ele é o maior que você pode encontrar, viu / você com a sua música esqueceu o principal / que no peito dos desafinados / no fundo do peito bate calado / que no peito dos desafinados também bate um coração." (But you mustn't speak this way of my love. It is the greatest you could find. You, with your music, have forgotten what is most important. In the chest of the out-of-tune, deep in the chest beating quietly, in the chest of the tuneless there also beats a heart.) Roughly a year after writing these timeless lyrics, Newton Mendonça died of a heart attack at age thirty-three. O, cruel irony.

What is it about "Desafinado" that seems out of tune? It is a subtle trick of Jobim's approach to the interplay of melody and harmony. The recording on *Getz/Gilberto* is in E-flat major, but the melody often stresses "borrowed" notes at the end of verse lines that are not in that scale. On the opening line, "Se você disser que eu desafino amor," the phrase initiates on the tonic chord, arriving at the dominant for the first syllable of *desafino* and both syllables of *amor*. Yet the B-flat of the tonic and dominant quickly slides into B-natural, the raised fifth or lowered-sixth interval, to complete the phrase. This B-natural creates a deliberate clash with both the tonic and dominant harmonies. The B-natural then becomes the lowered fifth of the following F7 chord, making it F7 b5. This creates a notable dissonance with the third of the chord. In the harmonic passage that begins with E-flat major 7 and ends with F7 b5, Jobim does not so much resolve dissonance as fold it into a complex harmonic progression.

Jobim employs a similar approach to the next line, "saiba que isto em mim provoca imensa dor." The line starts on Ab, then moves to D minor on the second syllable of *provoca*. On the last two syllables ('*sa dor*), the melody moves from D-flat major to E minor. Once again the sliding half-step creates dissonance. The fifth degree of the d minor sonority effects a lowered half-step (A natural to A-flat) then repeats the sequence, moving by root from D-natural to D-flat, minor to major sonority. Jobim takes it one step farther, ending the verse on an E minor sonority, moving downward from A-flat (of the D-flat major chord) to G natural or the third of E minor. The repeated half-step motion and modulations are unusual in popular music. It would take a listener with near perfect pitch to work this out on the basis of the recording alone (and that would not include the author of this book, who used sheet music).[1] But anyone whose ear is accustomed to the straight-ahead sounds of three-chord popular music—which is to say,

"Desafinado"

most of us—will *feel* that something is a little *different* here. These apparently dissonant notes continue throughout the composition, each time leading the listener into a new, more complex chord. That is the genius of Jobim, and of bossa nova more generally. It takes the listener into new terrain but does so through seduction rather than confrontation.

"Desafinado" is also unusual as popular music in its unitary structure—there is no alternation of verse and chorus. It is a complex piece of music, seventy-four measures long, with over twenty different chords in the harmony. In the original 1959 recording, Gilberto works through this structure once and then closes, bringing the recording in at slightly under two minutes. In the *Getz/Gilberto* recording, Gilberto plays and sings the structure once, then Getz solos over the structure once, followed by a brief coda. In contrast to most popular music, there is no obvious hook or repeated chorus. The apparently dissonant notes themselves serve as the hook: they catch the listener's ear and sustain attention through this unusually long structure.

Rhythmically, "Desafinado" is samba, and the melody conveys that samba rhythm perfectly, emphasizing samba syncopation. In Gilberto's renditions, that gives the interplay between voice and guitar an ineluctable propulsive power. On the *Getz/Gilberto* recording, the musicians play "Desafinado" at a slower tempo than the 1959 recording, a relaxed pace that allows the listener to catch Gilberto's subtle inflections. The *Getz/Gilberto* version includes Getz himself. He digs into Jobim's harmonies and phrasing, playing a sinuous solo that skirts around the melody, never rushing. Getz's solo contrasts clearly to his solo on his own 1962 recording—on *Getz/ Gilberto* he is more lyrical and restrained. He has transformed himself from a jazz musician playing bossa nova into a bossa nova musician. Jazz critics like Leonard Feather lamented this transformation, seeing that as a concession to popular music. Heard from another perspective, Getz has entered more fully into the spirit of the music and become *despojado*. As Getz riffs softly over the coda, Gilberto closes with an onomatopoetic vocal rendition of a samba beat, *dum-ti-bubum-ti-dum-ti-dum-dum*, a fittingly Gilbertian ending for this small, perfect marvel.

Figure 5 *Photograph by José Medeiros. Tom Jobim at the premiere of* Orfeu da Conceição, *September 1956. (Instituto Moreira Salles).*

12 The Cusp of Greatness

José Medeiros was one of Brazil's great photojournalists and cinematographers, and a privileged observer of Bossa Nova Rio. He captures Jobim on the cusp of greatness here. The image has the hallmarks of renaissance portraiture: a shaft of light illuminates the artist, and he looks toward the heavens with soulful eyes. The light shines brightest on his fine and delicate ear. Like his collaborator João Gilberto, Jobim could hear things that mere mortals could not. His harmonic innovation set the standard for all subsequent bossa nova composers. His six compositions on *Getz/Gilberto*, particularly "Desafinado" and "O Grande Amor," are excellent examples of his unique abilities.

This is a rare photograph of Jobim in a suit and tie. (Even Jobim had to dress for the Teatro Municipal.) On a more typical evening, he and Vinicius de Moraes might be found in short-sleeves at the Amarelinho, a sidewalk bar just across the square from the theater, drinking beer and trading in music and verse. Throughout his career, Jobim was famously easygoing. He drew inspiration from the sounds of nature, spending hours roaming the tropical splendor of Rio de Janeiro's Botanical Gardens listening to bird songs. Whenever his schedule allowed, he withdrew to a bucolic family retreat in the Atlantic rainforest outside of Rio.

One of the great ironies of *Getz/Gilberto* is that the notoriously irascible Getz and the standoffish and mercurial Gilberto combined to produce some of the loveliest music of the twentieth century. It could not have happened without the presence of the warm, companionable Jobim. It was Jobim who mediated between the two headliners. In his collegiality as well as his composition, he had a talent for turning apparent conflict into nuanced agreement.

13 "Corcovado"

Most English-language versions of bossa nova lyrics are disastrous. The original lyrics by figures like Vinicius de Moraes and Newton Mendonça captured the poetry of everyday Brazilian speech with rhythm and flair. The English versions, in contrast, tend toward the mundane, and often step clumsily on the rhythm in the process. Gene Lees was an exception, with an ear for Brazilian rhythm and an affinity for the sensibility of bossa nova. "Quiet Nights," his set of lyrics for Jobim's "Corcovado," was his first attempt at the form and his best known. The *Getz/Gilberto* recording, which pairs Astrud singing Lees's lyrics with João Gilberto singing Jobim's original Portuguese lyrics, forms a seamless whole.

Astrud begins, with delicate accompaniment from Jobim, while the rest of the band waits in the wings. "Quiet nights of quiet stars, quiet chords from my guitar, floating on the silence that surrounds us. Quiet thoughts and quiet dreams, quiet walks by quiet streams, and the window that looks out on Corcovado, oh how lovely." The repetition of *quiet*, ungainly on the page, is sonorous and inviting on the recording. Lees's version is not an exact translation of Jobim's original lyrics but captures their mood. And whereas Lees's original English version mentions only "the window that looks out on the mountain," Astrud gets more specific, singing "And the window that looks out on Corcovado, oh, how lovely."

That specificity is crucial, not only because it explains the song's title. Corcovado, the humpbacked hill, site of the massive statue of Christ the Redeemer that overlooks Rio de Janeiro, is the city's most iconic landmark. Corcovado and Christ the Redeemer are visible from most neighborhoods in Rio. This was even more true in 1960, before greater building heights obscured many views of Corcovado and urban sprawl reduced its constant presence as a geographic reference point. Both the original Portuguese lyrics and Lees's English version speak to Corcovado's centrality in carioca life, and reflect the importance of the natural landscape in Jobim's work.

For international listeners, Corcovado also represented the tropical exotic and its romantic possibilities. Many hearing Astrud Gilberto sing in 1964 would have vividly remembered the 1942 film *Now, Voyager*, in which repressed New England spinster Charlotte Vale (played by Bette Davis) embarks on a cruise to South America. The tropical delights of Rio de Janeiro draw Charlotte out of her shell, awakening her own sensuality. She tours Rio—including a spectacular visit to Corcovado—with dashing shipmate Jeremiah Duvaux Durrance (Paul Henreid), and they fall in love—a bittersweet awakening for Charlotte, as the pair must part ways. This was the promise of Rio for those who dreamed about it from afar—romance and temporary deliverance from the binding ties of work and family. It was a promise that Astrud Gilberto's sweet, unpretentious delivery seemed to represent.

After Astrud sings the first verse in English, Getz plays the bridge melody faithfully, and João sings the entire song in Portuguese. Getz returns for a more expansive solo, albeit one that remains fairly close to the melody, adding wistful, elegiac phrases. Jobim improvises over one verse, João returns to sing the second verse and the bridge, and Getz plays a lovely coda, delicately placing the lid back on the sugar jar.

As in the case of "Girl from Ipanema," the album recording clocked in too long for radio play, at 4:11. Taylor cut out João's first vocals for the shortened radio version. Depending on one's perspective, this was either a barbarous and craven capitulation to the market or a clever way to draw a broad radio audience to bossa nova, knowing many would end up buying the complete album, anyway. The radio version was largely forgotten, except by collectors. It is the full album version that endures and has become canonical.

"Corcovado"/"Quiet Nights" also became a jazz and cocktail lounge standard. It is included in many jazz "fake books," (compilations of sheet music that allow musicians to fake like they know the song). The English-language version has been recorded by an all-star list of jazz singers and cabaret crooners: Frank Sinatra, Sarah Vaughan, Nancy Wilson, Tony Bennett, Andy Williams, Diana Krall, Stacey Kent, Barbara Lewis, Laura Fygi, and John Pizzarelli. It has also been recorded by a more unexpected list of vocalists: Art Garfunkel, Marvin Gaye, Ch'Ella, Andrea Bocelli. Even Queen Latifah! There are remixes by DJs like Q-Function, and instrumental versions by jazz musicians like Ron Carter, Grant Green, and Oscar Peterson.

You could put "Quiet Nights" on Spotify to soothe you to sleep and still be hearing different versions when you woke up in the morning. That would take you through the easy-listening versions by artists like Engelbert Humperdinck, Perry Como, Percy Faith, and Doris Day. Is it surprising that Kenny G recorded "Quiet Nights"? No, it is not.

There are reasons this composition can appeal both to exacting jazz masters like Ron Carter and Oscar Peterson and to palliative "smooth jazz" artists like Kenny G: it has Jobim's nuanced changes, inviting open-ended improvisation. But its melody is more soothing than that of "Desafinado." It is a lovely lullaby. It is best when handled with care and restraint, as on *Getz/Gilberto*.

Figure 6 *Photo: José Medeiros. Ipanema, 1952. (Instituto Moreira Salles).*

14 Bossa Nova on the Car Radio

João Gilberto honed his approach to voice and guitar in a bathroom in Diamantina, but he could have used a Ford sedan. The acoustics would have been nearly as good. And Ford had been assembling cars in Brazil for decades. As poet Carlos Drummond de Andrade put it, "Eu também já fui brasileiro / moreno como vocês. / Ponteei viola, guiei forde / e aprendi na mesa dos bares / que o nacionalismo é uma virtude" (I also have been Brazilian, brown like you. I plucked a guitar, drove a Ford and learned at barroom tables that nationalism is a virtue).

Over the course of the 1950s the private automobile was transformed from a perquisite of the well-to-do to a staple of Brazil's growing middle class. And every private automobile was a concert hall built for two (or so), with a premium radio and powerful speakers. Plush sedans like those in the photograph even had padded panels in the cabin to limit noise from the outside world, allowing driver and passengers to hear every detail of the music coming over the airwaves.

Radio programming and romance changed accordingly. In the 1940s, Brazilian radio was characterized primarily by soap operas and live musical programs, often performed by a full orchestra in the studio. Flagship programs played lush arrangements of a wide variety of music for a family audience. Broadcasting recorded music was comparatively rare. (When Gilberto sang with a vocal quintet in Rio in the early 1950s, for example, they had a regular weekly slot for live performance on Rádio Tupi.) Toward the end of the 1950s, disc jockeys became common on Brazilian radio, just as bossa nova became Brazil's trendsetting popular music. The disc jockeys spun records of a certain type for a niche audience, with brief but knowing commentary between selections. Cool jazz and bossa nova were perfect for this approach. They were music meant for listening and connoisseurship, not dancing. Their target audience was young, acquisitive, and *pra frente*, to the front, or up-to-the-minute. And bossa nova records sounded great in the intimate environs of a Ford sedan.

The plush sedan became a favored location for romance, as well. What better date than to listen to João Gilberto singing just for the two of you while gazing out at the visual delights of Ipanema? In the foreground, the tall, tan, young and lovely. In the background, the glittering waves and a stretch of golden sand curving to Leblon, with the Dois Irmãos and Pedra da Gávea hills rising in the distance.

The license plate reads D.F., for Distrito Federal—Rio was still Brazil's national capital. It would remain the musical capital for many years. For the truly blessed, Bossa Nova Rio was a dream that existed. For as long as it endured, who would want to be anywhere else?

15 "Só Danço Samba"

"Só Danço Samba" means "I only dance samba." Norman Gimbel unfortunately saddled it with an English version whose title is "Jazz 'n' Samba," and it is often listed under that title, or simply as "Jazz Samba" in the United States. About Gimbel's English lyrics, the less said the better. We can be thankful they are not included on the *Getz/Gilberto* recording. Instead, we get a straightforward rendition of the original Jobim and de Moraes composition. Gilberto sings the verse, repeats it, sings the chorus, and repeats the verse again. Getz then blows through the same structure three times through, but with harmonic modulation, moving from D up to F, then up to Ab, before riffing over the coda and fading out.

Structurally and harmonically, "Só Danço Samba" is closer to swing than anything else on *Getz/Gilberto*. It has a thirty-two bar, AABA structure (verse, verse, chorus, verse), the canonical form for swing. The melody on the verse consists primarily of a series of repeated two-note phrases in samba rhythm, and lends itself to finger-poppin' rendition. Not surprisingly, this is the song where Getz draws most deeply on the jazz saxophone tradition. In contrast to the other compositions, where he stays fairly close to the melody, on "Só Danço Samba" he diverges from the start, ripping through a series of blues and bebop-inflected phrases, as the rhythm section pushes him along. Only on his third passage through the structure does he offer a relatively faithful statement of the melody. As he does so, Banana alters his accompaniment, adding to the ambience by subtracting the brushes, as if in order to display the melody in high relief. On the coda, Getz gets as bluesy as he is likely to get before closing with a more typically lyrical phrase. Gilberto, Neto, and Banana remain locked in a groove throughout. Jobim keeps his own participation on piano as spare as imaginable, outside a John Cage performance.

This is Jobim at his simplest as a composer. De Moraes, as always, takes his cue from the composer. If the first verse works, why bother with a second? Just repeat as necessary. "Só danço samba, só danço samba, vai vai vai vai vai. Só danço samba, só danço samba. Vai." (I only dance samba, I only dance samba, go go go go go. I only dance samba, I only dance samba, go.) One studying these lyrics in isolation might be misled into thinking de Moraes is less than a towering genius of Brazilian song. But they serve the melody perfectly. The chorus gets more adventurous: "Já dancei twist até demais. Mas não sei, me cansei, do calypso e cha cha cha." (I already danced the Twist, maybe too much. But I don't know, I got tired of calypso and cha cha cha.)

Unlike some of the exalted nationalist samba of the 1940s, the nativism here is tongue-in-cheek. The pronounced jazz elements of the composition make it clear that the lyrics are the vain assertions of one who doth protest too much. If anything, the lyrics show just how closely attuned Rio's hipsters were to changing trends in the United States, keeping up with the cha

cha cha craze of the second half of the 1950s. (In his English version, by contrast, Gimbel took the literalist route, explaining the combination of jazz and samba in case anyone missed the point—while simultaneously scrubbing his lyrics clean of swing and syncopation.)

Like Getz, Gilberto uses the simplicity of the verse melody as an invitation to greater rhythmic variation, charging out in front of the beat on the third statement of the verse. He can place the notes wherever he likes. He is unstoppable. And he always swings.

Figure 7 *Photograph by José Medeiros. Tom Jobim and Vinicius de Moraes collaborate, 1956. (Instituto Moreira Salles).*

16 Happiness Is a Drop of Dew

French film director Marcel Camus knew he wanted to make a film version of *Orfeu da Conceição*. But Conceição, so richly evocative for the audience in Rio de Janeiro, would mean nothing to an international audience. Camus called his version *Orfeu Negro* (Black Orpheus) instead. And he wanted new music. Some say Camus's French producers did not want to pay royalties to Brazilian publishing companies, so they insisted on new material that could be copyrighted in France. This seems unlikely, given lax international copyright standards for popular music in the period. Brazilian copyrights had not stopped Hollywood from borrowing Brazilian material and avoiding royalties, for example. It seems more likely that Camus wanted music that would ride the cresting wave that would soon be known as bossa nova.

Jobim and de Moraes complied, as did Luiz Bonfá. Jobim and de Moraes wrote "A Felicidade" (Happiness) for *Black Orpheus*, and produced an arrangement that balances bossa nova on the verse with Carnival samba on the chorus. It is among their most beautiful collaborations, which became a bossa nova standard. De Moraes's lyrics emphasize the transitory nature of happiness, and the enduring legacy of sadness. "A felicidade é uma gota de orvalho numa petala de flor. . . ." (Happiness is a drop of dew on a flower petal). Bonfá also rose to the occasion, composing "Manhã de Carnaval" (Carnival Morning), the song that would become the film's calling card, and by far the best known of Bonfá's prolific career.

Camus's 1959 film presented a more folkloric vision of the favela than did de Moraes's original play. Brazilian viewers derided its stereotyped notions of exotic Rio. But Camus also shot hours of footage at Rio's Carnival for the film. Cringeworthy moments notwithstanding, *Black Orpheus* includes a six-minute, uninterrupted scene of Rio's Carnival parade that remains one of the most valuable documents of 1950s Carnival samba. And the soundtrack is among the greatest in the history of film. In bringing bossa nova to an international audience, it helped pave the way for *Getz/Gilberto*.

Figure 8 *Photograph by José Medeiros. Mercedes Batista and Valter Ribeiro dance at the Gafieira Estudantina, 1956. (Instituto Moreira Salles).*

17 Dancehall Memories

Bossa nova was not dance music. At least not in Rio. The music emerged from two kinds of spaces, neither of which featured dancing. The first were the *inferninhos*, or crowded, tiny nightclubs of Copacabana, where tables were packed so tightly that waiters could barely make their way through without spilling the whiskey. The second were the living rooms of upper-middle-class Ipanema, particularly that of the family of singer Nara Leão, where the bossa crowd converged and collaborated in the late 1950s.

Brazilian composers and performers were disappointed if not surprised when US marketers created a ballroom bossa nova dance in 1962. Every prior Latin music craze in the United States had a dance to go with it, from the *maxixe* of the 1910s to the *cha-cha-cha* of the late 1950s. Marketers felt bossa would only take off in the United States if it had its own dance. Brazilians, as well as cool jazz adepts of the form like Gerry Mulligan, saw it as an abomination. In 1963, Gene Lees published an article in *Downbeat* entitled, "Bossa Nova: Anatomy of a Travesty." Lees lamented the spoliation of the genre by marketers in both Brazil and the United States. He quoted Jobim saying, "Bossa nova is not a dance. We do not dance to it in Brazil. It is a music to listen to, like good jazz. But now they have a bossa nova dance in the United States, and I see they have here bossa nova shoes."[1]

We liked bossa before it was cool, hipsters like Mulligan and Lees indicated. Remember, this was *before* the release of *Getz/Gilberto*, which came to define bossa nova for most global listeners. *Getz/Gilberto* was recorded one month after Lees's article appeared in *Downbeat*.

Bossa nova may not have been a dance in Brazil. But it was only one step removed from the *gafieiras* of Rio de Janeiro. *Gafieiras* are unpretentious dance-halls. The music is mostly samba, but samba is designed for couples dancing in close embrace, unlike Carnival samba. Most bossa nova musicians played in *gafieira* bands at one time or another—they were in an excellent place to learn the repertoire of Brazilian popular music, and to develop the chops of a gigging musician. Throughout his career, one of João Gilberto's favorite songs to play was "Sem Compromisso" (No Commitment), a 1950s samba by Geraldo Pereira. The narrator of "Sem Compromisso" laments that his date has abandoned him at the *gafieira* and insists on dancing with another man. Gilberto's version takes the eminently danceable syncopation of the Geraldo Pereira composition and distills it into a voice and guitar performance. Gilberto may not have intended it for dancing, but the ghost of *gafieira* dance moves within it.

The photograph shows the celebrated dancers Mercedes Batista and Valter Ribeiro at Estudantina, Rio's best-known *gafieira*. The dancehall is simple, with minimal decoration. Chairs line the walls for those waiting for their next dance. For now, Ribeiro and Batista own the floor, a portrait of elegance and panache. At the time the photo was taken, Batista was the only black dancer in the regular corps at the Teatro Municipal. She was a frequent collaborator of Abdias do Nascimento's Black Experimental Theater group, and went to found her own Afro-Brazilian dance company.

It bears noting that the *gafieiras* were one of the most integrated spaces in 1950s Rio. The rhetoric of racial democracy reflected aspirations, rather than reality, at best. Elite spaces were still reserved for white Brazilians through unspoken social codes, and blackness correlated heavily with poverty. But racial mixture was not a myth, and there were places where it flourished in ways that came closest to realizing the aspirations of racial democracy. The *gafieiras*, where dancers, musicians, and waitstaff all reflected Brazil's racial diversity, were among the most important. Bossa nova, one step removed from the gafieiras, was also one step removed from their flourishing integration. But the genre bore their influence, nevertheless.

18 "O Grande Amor"

"O Grande Amor" (The Great Love) is the second masterpiece on the album, after "Desafinado." It is not one of Jobim's best-known or celebrated works, perhaps because of its unremarkable title, easily confused with any number of other songs about great love, perhaps because it lacks the kind of pop hook that vaulted "Girl from Ipanema" to global familiarity. It has nonetheless been recorded dozens of times, by performers ranging from hard-bop pianist Mulgrew Miller to Russian crooner Irina Zemtsova. No subsequent version, however, approaches the *Getz/Gilberto* recording for crystalline perfection.

Like "Desafinado," it is a composition of harmonic daring in an atypical format for popular song. It is unitary in structure—there is no alternation of verse and chorus. There is just one, achingly tender, isometric poem set to a brooding melody and a subtle harmony, thirty-two bars long. In both structure and mood, it is an aria not a pop song. Jobim was an erudite composer before the birth of bossa nova, and this song, more than any other on the album, bears the hallmarks of his training with Hans Joachim Koellreutter. This is the kind of composition Jobim was referring to when he remarked to a colleague, "We've fooled them. They think we are making popular music."

Getz starts the recording off, and his timbre is ethereal and supple but still precise. He opens with an ascending perfect fourth (E to A), then plays the descending melodic line as Jobim composed it, with few embellishments. The melody is set in A Aeolian mode (or the A natural minor scale), then modulates to D Aeolian (or the D natural minor scale) before returning to A. But, as with all great bossa nova, there is something more subtle going on. The Aeolian mode is nearly ubiquitous in minor-key popular music, and "O Grande Amor" seems to start out in this direction. But it takes some unexpected side-steps along the way. "O Grande Amor" hinges on repeated use of a G#, both in the melody and in the bass—a note not heard in pure A Aeolian mode. This is a crucial part of what gives the song its quality of ineffable resignation, rather than simple melancholy.

In contrast to the melody, the harmony is richly chromatic. Where the melody descends mostly in whole step motion, the harmony moves in half-steps, passing through chords that extend the harmonic palette. The harmony begins with A minor, moves down a half-step to G# diminished, then down another half-step to G minor 6. Similarly, as the melody modulates from D Aeolian back to A Aeolian, the harmony moves from D minor 7 to D# diminished to A minor with an E in the bass. The melody does not clash with the harmony, but nor does it slide easily within it, hand-in-glove. Instead, as in most great bossa nova, there is a tension between melody and harmony. The melody can sound like it is veering toward dissonance, when it is the harmonic sands that are shifting underneath it.[1] Jobim plays the first eight measures of the harmony as broken chords, one note at a time. After eight bars, Gilberto begins his trademark guitar batida, locking into a down-tempo rhythm with Neto and Banana.

Rhythmically, too, "O Grande Amor" conveys a certain tension, moving back and forth between stress on the first beat of the measure to syncopated phrases floating across two or three measures in counter-rhythm. The melody begins on the beat, then slides toward syncopation. And in contrast to "Só Danço Samba," where Gilberto as vocalist plays with the rhythm, in the case of "O Grande Amor" he remains faithful to Jobim's score. Indeed, "O Grande Amor" is a vivid example of Gilberto's tremendous tonal and rhythmic control.

Gilberto sings the song once, then Getz returns with a deft, lyrical improvisation, probing the tension between melody and harmony. Jobim follows with a typically understated improvisation of his own, carefully choosing his notes as if to emphasize certain elements within the harmony. Getz returns for another pass, building to a valedictory phrase that resolves harmonically without quite dispelling the sorcery. This rich interplay of melody, harmony, and rhythm, and the subtle tension between them, are part of what give great bossa its depth and allure.

Then there is the poem itself:

Haja o que houver
Há sempre um homem para uma mulher
E há de sempre haver para esquecer
Um falso amor, e uma vontade de morrer
Seja como for, há de vencer o grande amor

Que há de ser no coração
Como um perdão pra quem chorou

[Come what may
There is always a man for a woman
And there must always be, in order to forget,
A false love, and a desire to die.
No matter what, great love must triumph
It must come into the heart
Like a pardon for those who wept.]

This is classic de Moraes: spare, almost conversational, but not simple. The first line is almost deliberately trite, and then suddenly we plunge into the depths of false love and a desire to die. These lyrics come precisely as the melody modulates from A Aeolian to D Aeolian, pulling us down while the harmonic ground shifts beneath us. The triumph of great love and the pardon for those who wept then arrive on the return to A Aeolian, concluding with an A in the melody over E7(b9) in the harmony, a note that leads into and sustains throughout the A minor 7 in the next measure. In the context of the lyrics, this is a musical resolution that feels like redemption.

Figure 9 *Photograph by José Medeiros. Haroldo Costa and cast in rehearsals for* Orfeu da Conceição, 1956. *(Instituto Moreira Salles).*

19 Haroldo Costa as Orfeu

The multitalented singer, musician, and actor Haroldo Costa played the title role in *Orfeu da Conceição*. Costa went on to have a long and successful career in Brazilian film, music, and television. But like all the black members of the original cast, his career was also limited by the racial structures of Brazil's entertainment industry. After Orfeu, lead roles would be few and far between, even for an actor as talented as Costa. The dancer in the lower-left foreground seems to see it all coming—the promise and the disillusionment, the opportunity and the limitation. She knows the score before the game has even been played.

Literary and cultural studies scholar David Treece identifies the inherent tension of unfulfilled promises as essential to bossa nova, manifest in everything from the girl from Ipanema who will never fulfill the narrator's desire to the "syncopation, oscillating melodic figures and dissonance" within the music. Treece argues that this "dynamic tension" is most evident in notions of time in bossa nova, "its tension between the mythic, ritual time of the eternal return, and the quotidian time of the contemporary city."[1]

The role Costa is playing, that of Orfeu, is bound by the mythic, ritual time of the eternal return. The gaze of the dancer in the foreground is wise to the ways of the contemporary city. It was in bossa nova's nature to leave certain matters unresolved.

20 Olga Albizu and "Alla Africa"

The cover features a reproduction of the Olga Albizu painting "Alla Africa" set against a black field, with **GETZ/GILBERTO** at the top in pale orange, followed by the full names of the two leaders in smaller type, in bright orange (first STAN GETZ, then JOAO GILBERTO, with no tilde over the *a* for poor João). And in smaller type yet again, in lower case, but in bright yellow, "featuring Antonio Carlos Jobim." The Verve record label logo is in the lower left. But most of the cover space is dedicated to the reproduction of Albizu's painting.

Albizu was a Puerto Rican abstract expressionist living in New York. She had already become one of the favored artists for RCA and Verve album covers, with her work featured on seven records before *Getz/Gilberto*. Creed Taylor had produced the last three of those, all nominally in the jazz samba or bossa nova vein, starting with Getz and Charlie Byrd's *Jazz Samba* from early 1962. After the unexpected success of *Jazz Samba*, Taylor created a series of jazz samba/bossa nova albums, and used Albizu's work to brand the series, giving it a coherent visual identity. Taylor followed *Jazz Samba* with Getz's *Big Band Bossa Nova* from late 1962, and Getz and Luiz Bonfá's *Jazz Samba Encore* from 1963. The Albizu covers for all the albums in the series (including *Getz/Gilberto* and *Getz/Gilberto vol. 2*) are similar works of roughly rectangular slabs of pigment applied thickly to the canvas with a spatula, swimming on a monochromatic background.

Getz/Gilberto is the most visually arresting of the series: the oranges and yellows of "Alla Africa" pop against the black field, while the black slabs echo that field. The three preceding covers were relatively cool in palette: *Jazz Samba* is mostly magenta on a white field. *Big Band Bossa Nova* is mostly mustard on a pale yellow field. *Jazz Samba Encore* is mostly light blue on a white field. All were part of a trend of cool abstract expressionist covers for cool jazz albums of the late 1950s and early 1960s. The palette for "Alla Africa," in contrast, is hot—bright orange and brilliant yellow, colors that promise sensual heat rather than cerebral cool. The cover was crucial to the album's success. It was nominated for a Grammy for best album cover of the year and was one of the most instantly recognizable covers in a decade when album cover art was at a peak of creativity and influence.

Like Astrud Gilberto, Albizu came to the project by chance. Albizu (b.1924) was from a relatively wealthy family in Puerto Rico, but when she moved to New York in 1948 she was a struggling art student. She lived in International House, the quasi-dormitory for international students adjacent to Columbia University, and took art classes at the Hans Hoffman School of Arts, a hotbed of abstract expressionism. As a Latina woman, Albizu found it doubly difficult to crack the insular male world of the downtown art scene. But as an abstract expressionist, she had little in common with the figurative, activist art celebrated among Puerto Rican artists in East Harlem. Albizu was caught between East Harlem and Greenwich Village, between abstract expressionist and Latin American art scenes. As art historian Abigail McEwen puts it, "In between the downtown scene of the aging New York School and its progeny and the Nuyorican movement in upper Manhattan, Albizu worked in a private no-(wo)man's-land."[1]

In the 1950s, Albizu worked as a secretary at RCA to make ends meet. Adele Siegal, one of her friends at RCA, hung several of Albizu's paintings on her office walls. They came to the attention of George Marek, head of the RCA Records Division, and Bob Jones, his art director. Jones featured Albizu works on three classical albums of the 1950s. Albizu's first cover for Verve was for a 1961 cool jazz big-band album by the Bob Brookmeyer Orchestra. From Brookmeyer to Getz was a small step. Taylor knew he wanted abstract art for *Jazz Samba*, and someone at Verve proposed Albizu. As Taylor remembers it, "The image looked perfect. It didn't make any particular statement about what a jazz samba was, because there was no jazz samba until *Jazz Samba*. There was no preexisting graphic image to go with it."[2]

Taylor exaggerated the novelty of the musical approach: even leaving aside combinations of samba and jazz that had been common in Brazil for several years, Laurindo Almeida and Bud Shank's *Brazilliance* had put jazz samba on the US jazz map in 1954. But Taylor was correct that abstract expressionism was the right choice for the Getz series on Verve. The indeterminacy and open-ended nature of the images reflected the music.

Olga Albizu and "Alla Africa"

"Alla Africa," in particular, was appropriate for *Getz/Gilberto*. It is hard not to see the vivid but unresolved nature of Albizu's work as analogous to Jobim's harmonies, reflecting similar positions between artistic worlds (Jobim between popular and erudite, Brazil and Europe, Albizu between Latin American and abstract expressionist). In McEwen's words, "Albizu's painting chafed against these art-historical narratives—Puerto Rican, Latin American, American—and her mode of abstract expressionism may be . . . understood as a border practice, enacted at the internal and external limits of national and cultural (and again, gendered) identity."[3]

Border practice is a good term for the music on *Getz/Gilberto* as well, crossing borders of United States and Brazil, Portuguese and English, jazz and samba, in ways that leave distinctions unresolved. Even the title of Albizu's work harmonizes with the concerns of bossa nova: "Alla Africa," which can be rendered as *a la Africa*, in Spanish, or "to Africa." Bossa nova existed in tension between the Afro-Brazilian roots of samba and the middle-class and largely white background of most of its performers. Albizu's work exists in tension between the cerebral world of abstract expressionism and the Afro-Latin source material indicated in the title. The inclusion of Albizu's work may have been partly the work of chance, but it was perfectly in sync with the spirit of the album.

Figure 10 *Photograph by José Medeiros. Ipanema, 1950s. (Instituto Moreira Salles).*

21 Two, Three, Many Girls from Ipanema

When the seventeenth-century Dutch painter Albert Eckhout came to Brazil, he created paintings designed to show the natural bounty of the exotic land. Images of Brazilian fertility, sensuality, and natural abundance were already well established in Europe: In the first letter from Brazil, written in 1500, Portuguese navigator Pero Vaz de Caminha described it as a land "where everything grows and flourishes." He also emphasized that indigenous women "have no shame." Subsequent chroniclers would largely reproduce Caminha's exotic vision, and Eckhout was no exception.

Among Eckhout's most striking images is one of a Tapuia indigenous woman, naked but for a few strategically placed tropical leaves, with a basket of severed body parts slung over her shoulder. In her right hand, she holds a severed arm, and gives the impression that she may start snacking on it if she gets peckish. It is among the more lurid and fantastical images inspired by the fifteenth- and sixteenth-century reports of cannibalism among the indigenous populations of the Brazilian coast. In the background of the painting, through the Tapuia woman's legs, one can see a line of Tapuia warriors walking down a hillside. It is as if the Tapuia woman is symbolically giving birth to her kin through the act of ritual cannibalism.

Flash forward to Ipanema beach in the 1950s. Photographer José Medeiros captures the legs and waists of two women in the foreground, framing the sunbathing beauty that lies between them. Through the legs of one of standing women, we see another girl from Ipanema rising from the waves. Is that another in the distance? They seem to proliferate before our eyes.

There is no evidence of cannibalism in the photograph. But in the same period the Portuguese verb *comer*, to eat, became slang for *to have sex*. In the brave new world of intrepid little sprouts, to fornicate was to consume, an act that could be initiated by women as well as men. Bossa Nova Rio merely hinted at these social transformations in the late 1950s. It would take another decade or so before they substantially reshaped gender codes and expectations in Brazil.

Getz/Gilberto

22 "Vivo Sonhando"

"Vivo Sonhando" is the only composition on the album with both music and lyrics by Jobim. He is known primarily as one of the twentieth century's great composers, but he was proficient as a lyricist, as well. The classic "Águas de Março," for example, is one of the great examples of popular song in the format of a list, running through a catalogue of flotsam and jetsam washed up by Rio's March rains. The gorgeous love song "Luiza," with lyrics by the composer, builds inexorably toward a marvelous evocation of romantic ecstasy, with melody, harmony, and lyrics perfectly matched.

"Vivo Sonhando" is not one of those cases. The lyrics are comparatively mundane, the quiet muttering of poor soul longing for a love who does not arrive, leaving him lonely and gazing at the moon. The harmony goes through a series of intricate chord changes as the lyrics evoke "a time to speak of the stars, the sea, love, the moon" (the imaginary world of bossa nova, always just out of reach). This opens a range of possibilities for Getz as improviser, and he breezes through three choruses, playing rhythmic phrases as Gilberto and company keep the rhythm pulsing. On his vocals, Gilberto gives the lyrics an intimacy that avoids overloading them with sentiment. And Milton Banana, who faithfully plays a supporting role throughout the album, allows himself slightly more variation on "Vivo Sonhando," giving greater indication of what can be done with tasteful bossa percussion. But the song's importance on *Getz/Gilberto* seems to be primarily to close the album with something less weighty than "O Grande Amor." "Vivo Sonhando," by contrast, is almost blithe.

Figure 11 *Photograph by José Medeiros. Bicycles on the beach, Rio de Janeiro, 1950s.*

23 Bossa and Bicycles

Bossa Nova Rio was a place where you could leave your bicycle unlocked in a beachside rack, come back at the end of the day and find it still there. It was a place where you could ride a bicycle with a sidecar and expect your passenger not to get clipped by a bus, truck, or taxi on the way to the beach. It would be hard to believe it if we did not have the photographs. It is said that those who grew up watching Pelé play for Santos in these same years developed unnatural expectations of soccer excellence, and emerged with a severely distorted vision of what is possible in the real world. It is possible that those who heard João Gilberto, Tom Jobim, Vinicius de Moraes, and cohort inventing bossa nova experienced a similar phenomenon. The Rio de Janeiro they inhabited in the late 1950s would not last long, alas.

24 Afterlife of the Girl from Ipanema

Verve records released the truncated radio version of "Girl from Ipanema" in February 1964, and added the full *Getz/Gilberto* to its catalog of new releases for the year. As with many details about the album's production, it is not entirely clear why Creed Taylor and Verve waited nearly a year after the recording session to release the album. Ruy Castro, author of the most extensive history of bossa nova, suggests that Castro believed the bossa nova craze was already in rapid decline. With little hope for success, he was in no rush to release the record. Taylor himself remembered it differently, indicating he knew he had a hit on his hands when he recorded Astrud Gilberto: "The surprise was when Astrud came in with her little voice to sing the lyric with that accent. I knew the song was going to be an absolute smash. You would have to be deaf and totally out of it not to hear that."[1]

It seems most likely that Taylor and Verve were biding their time, waiting for the most propitious moment. They chose wisely: "Girl from Ipanema" shot up the Billboard singles chart to number five. *Getz/Gilberto* rose to number two on the album chart, and stayed on the charts for ninety-six weeks, unprecedented for a jazz record. Getz, Gilberto, Jobim, and

Astrud were suddenly hot properties in the entertainment world. They could not tour together, however, as they had already gone their separate ways. Jobim had pressing engagements in Rio de Janeiro shortly after the *Getz/Gilberto* sessions: future collaborations with Creed Taylor would have to wait. João and Astrud Gilberto embarked on a European tour in mid-1963, along with Tião Neto, Milton Banana, and the pianist João Donato. During an extended stay in Italy, João and Astrud split, months before the release of "Girl from Ipanema."

João Gilberto traveled to Paris for a club engagement, and happened to meet Miúcha Buarque de Holanda, a Brazilian who was studying Art History at the Louvre and singing in a café at night. When João came back to New York in 1964, Miúcha came with him. The couple were married the following year. Miúcha began her professional singing career simultaneously, and began performing with João, making future performances with João and Astrud together unlikely.

Taylor did manage to get João, Astrud, and Stan Getz together for one concert, on October 9, 1964, playing a mix of bossa nova and ballads. Taylor and Verve released the songs that did *not* feature Astrud as *Getz/Gilberto vol.2* in 1965. You can't catch lightning in a bottle twice. *Getz/Gilberto vol.2* was neither a commercial nor a critical success.

The selections featuring Astrud Gilberto did not fare much better. Taylor and Verve released them on a late 1964 album entitled *Getz Au Go Go*, along with a few selections recorded at a previous concert, without João Gilberto. *Getz Au Go Go* demonstrated Astrud's ability to handle American songbook standards like the Rodgers and Hammerstein ballad "It Might as Well Be Spring," but it did not attract anything close to the enthusiasm of *Getz/Gilberto*. It lacked the magic.

A series of television and film performances throughout 1964 were more important in building Astrud Gilberto's brand. Her performance of "Girl from Ipanema" in the 1964 MGM film *Get Yourself a College Girl* is indicative. The film's plot follows a group of female undergraduates from California on a ski vacation to Sun Valley, Idaho. One of the undergraduates is also a songwriter, and her connection to the music industry serves as the plot device justifying musical performances by groups including the Dave Clark Five, the Standells, the Animals, and Jimmy Smith, encompassing doo-wop, rock, and organ-trio jazz-blues. Bossa nova is merely part of the potpourri.

At the start of the scene, the camera pans left to right across a Sun Valley lodge filled with beautiful coeds in incongruous summer attire, as fake snow falls in the background. Getz's band of young US jazz musicians, including vibraphonist Gary Burton, plays the opening chords to "Girl from Ipanema." We hear Astrud before we see her. She is hiding behind a copy of the sheet music for the song, which serves simultaneously as an announcement of the title, an advertisement, and the curtain for Astrud's big reveal. She pulls the sheet music back just as she reaches "each one she passes goes ahh" in the lyrics. Astrud wears a pale-blue sundress with a matching bow in her teased hair. As she crosses stage right, Getz nods appreciatively, if a bit smugly. He is a vision of 1960s country club style in light-blue cardigan and oxford, matching Astrud's palette.

Sun Valley is culturally and geographically about as far from Ipanema as one can get, but the fantasy of sensual abundance transfers smoothly. The camera cuts to the audience: all young women, wearing a bizarre combination of heels and leotards. It looks more like a casting call for a Bob Fosse production than a ski lodge. Two, three, many girls from Sun Valley. Astrud remains cool and remote, pleasant but not trying hard to please. The audience can come to her if it likes. When she finishes, the young women applaud, and the jazz musicians nod knowingly.

Get Yourself a College Girl helped set the tone for the afterlife of "Girl From Ipanema." While Bonfá's "Manhã de Carnaval" was becoming a jazz standard, "Girl from Ipanema" became a pop standard. Most versions tended toward easy-listening banality. It became the song serious jazz fans tried in vain to get out of their head. "Girl from Ipanema" elevator music became a running gag of film and television. Showing characters standing awkwardly in an elevator while a lush string and synthesizer version of the song tootles in the background was an easy way to intersperse a brief moment of comic relief in action or drama films. The classic elevator scene in *Blues Brothers*, for example, shows Jake and Elwood Blues calmly riding an excruciatingly slow elevator, serenaded by a bland version of "Girl from Ipanema," intercut with footage of the heavily armed forces of the Chicago police, the National Guard, and various other forces rushing madly to apprehend or destroy them. More interestingly, many of these movies are about confidence games and other smooth liars. (*Catch Me if You Can, The Thomas Crown Affair, Mr. Nice, Nice Guys, Color of Money, Mr. and Mrs. Smith*.)[2] Even when ostensibly used as the material of a deliberately trite gag, something about the song's combination of alluring surface and subtle depths seemed particularly appropriate for stories of deceptive charm.

Astrud Gilberto received the minimum wage for a session musician for her work on the original recording. She had no stake in the royalties. But she used the song as the launching pad for a successful career, achieving greater stability in that regard than either Getz or Gilberto. She spent most of that career in New York, headlining at jazz clubs like the Blue Note and Sweet Basil's, and playing the European summer festival circuit. She always had a great backing band, chose her material wisely, and knew how to leave an audience wanting more. Over years of working the clubs, she developed considerable technical proficiency without ever feeling the need to show off her chops. Anyone who continues to doubt her technique can set those doubts to rest by listening to her 1987 work, *Astrud Gilberto Plus the James Last Orchestra*, where she demonstrates her ability to sing challenging material with grace and control. She largely retired on her own terms in the early 2000s.

Jobim was already Brazil's most prominent active composer before *Getz/Gilberto*, and he retained that prominence until his death in 1994, when he went straight to the pantheon. He became predominantly identified with the genre he helped create, but his career was bigger than bossa nova. He worked in every idiom of Brazilian music and brought his inimitable genius to each. Choros like Jobim's "Radamés e Pelé" and soundtracks like the one he wrote for the 1985 Globo television miniseries *O Tempo e o Vento* are masterpieces of their respective forms.

Most of Jobim's career unfolded within Brazil, but he continued to tour internationally and to record occasionally in the United States. While he clearly preferred to spend his days either on his family's hideaway in the lush Atlantic forest or strolling in Rio de Janeiro's Botanical Garden, success in the United States and the ability to harness the power of its recording industry remained crucial to his career. His 1967 collaboration with Frank Sinatra, recorded in Los Angeles, was one prominent example. But several other Jobim classics were also recorded in the United States, even though they lacked participation of headlining US musicians. The 1974 album *Elis & Tom*, with Jobim teaming up with singer Elis Regina, for example, was also recorded in Los Angeles. Many bossaphiles consider *Elis & Tom* the greatest bossa nova record.

Not all Jobim's US recordings became well known, but some deserve greater renown. This is particularly true of the Creed Taylor–produced album *Stone Flower* of 1970. Jobim and Taylor recorded at sound engineer Rudy Van Gelder's studio, in Englewood Cliffs, New Jersey, with an assemblage of cutting-edge Brazilian musicians and experienced jazz musicians. *Stone Flower* is Jobim's underappreciated masterpiece. The compositions, arrangements, and performances are gorgeous. The recording quality and sound engineering are, if anything, even better than *Getz/Gilberto*. Van Gelder had an unrivaled ability to create a sense of physical space in his recordings, and each instrument on *Stone Flower* sounds warm and distinct. It is easy to understand why *Getz/Gilberto vol.2* and *Getz Au Go Go* did not take off: they are not very good records. *Stone Flower*, in contrast, is a *great* record, but attracted even less attention. It has Jobim and Taylor at their best, but lacks the star quality of João and Astrud Gilberto, as well as that of Getz. It presents a different kind of counterexample to *Getz/Gilberto*, a reminder of just how many ingredients fell perfectly into place to make that album iconic.

Getz and João Gilberto were both brilliant musicians with difficult personalities, and each spent his later career tormented by his own kind of demons. Getz experimented with jazz fusion in the 1970s, then returned to bossa nova, recording with João Gilberto and Miúcha. For the remainder of his career, bossa nova seemed to be something he could not afford to abandon, despite his inclinations. His personal life remained turbulent. Acrimonious divorces are hardly newsworthy in the world of professional music, but Getz's divorce from Monica Silfverskiöld Getz was in a category apart, playing out in the courts over more than a decade, while both parties slid toward financial insolvency. (Following Getz's death in 1991, Silfverskiöld Getz drew on the painful experience to found a non-profit advocating for systemic change in divorce and family court.)

João Gilberto spent most of the 1960s and 1970s outside of Brazil, recording several great albums (*João Gilberto en México* of 1970, *João Gilberto* of 1973, and *Amoroso* of 1977) while also establishing a reputation as one of the most exacting and mercurial performers in the business. He returned to Brazil in 1980, but became increasingly remote over the next two decades. As in Getz's case, Gilberto's later years have been dominated by a protracted, bitter legal struggle. Gilberto sued recording company EMI for the rights to the master recordings of his first three albums, recorded in Brazil in the late 1950s. As in *Getz v Getz*, Gilberto's children from his first two marriages became embroiled in the case, to the enduring frustration of all, with no satisfying resolution. In the process, Gilberto lost touch with most of his former collaborators and avoided his admirers, becoming increasingly hermetic. Not even a late-blooming love affair and new fatherhood in his seventies could reverse his increasing isolation. As this book goes to press, news circulates of an aging Gilberto in a state of penury, hounded by debts, lawsuits, health problems, and family conflict.

What about the girl from Ipanema herself? Helô Pinheiro, acknowledged by both de Moraes and Jobim as the inspiration for the song (at least in part), became a minor celebrity in her own right. In this case, the lawsuit was more the cause of the celebrity than its decline. Pinheiro opened a boutique in Ipanema called "A Garota de Ipanema." The composers' heirs, owners of the copyright to the song, sued Pinheiro for infringement in 2001. The lawsuit propelled Pinheiro from relative obscurity to international public favor, and greatly contributed to her recognition as the inspiration for the song.

Rua Montenegro, where Pinheiro inspired Jobim and de Moraes, was renamed Rua Vinicius de Moraes. Rio's international airport was renamed after Jobim, perhaps in homage to his "Samba do Avião," or Airplane Samba. Bossa Nova Rio is long gone. Rio de Janeiro is now known more as the location of the violent gang wars of *City of God* than of the poetic bliss of "Corcovado." It was fleeting, but Bossa Nova Rio was more than an illusion. Its legacy is still with us, in *Getz/Gilberto* and the larger body of unforgettable music it represents.

Notes

Chapter 1

1 The most complete history of bossa nova is by Ruy Castro, *Chega de Saudade: a história e as histórias de bossa nova* (São Paulo: Companhia das Letras, 1990). For Castro's summary of Getz/Gilberto in particular, see Castro, "Anatomia de um disco," *Revista Brasileiros*, June 26, 2008. Sérgio Cabral has written the most extensive biography of Jobim, including an illuminating review of Jobim's collaboration with João Gilberto. Sérgio Cabral, *Antonio Carlos Jobim, uma biografia* (Rio de Janeiro: Lumiar, 1997). For a collection of articles and essays on various aspects of João Gilberto's career, see Walter Garcia, *João Gilberto* (São Paulo: Cosac Naify, 2012).

Chapter 2

1 Cabral, *Antonio Carlos Jobim, uma biografia;* Marc Fischer, *À Procura de João Gilberto* (São Paulo: Companhia das Letras, 2011); Daniella Thompson, "Plain João: the Man Who Invented Bossa," *Música Brasiliensis*, May 1998, http://daniellathompson.com/Texts/Brazzil/Plain_Joao.htm

2 João Gilberto's guitar batida has been extensively analyzed. For a brief, clear, and careful description, see Suzel Reily, "Tom Jobim and the bossa nova era," *Popular Music* 15, no. 1 (1996): 12–13.

3 For analysis of Gilberto's restraint, see Carlo Machado Pianta, "A Gênese da Bossa Nova: João Gilberto e Tom Jobim," dissertação de mestrado, Letras, UFRGS, Porto Alegre, 2010.

4 Cabral, *Antonio Carlos Jobim*, 132.

Chapter 3

1 Lydia Hutchison, "The Story Behind 'The Girl from Ipanema,'" *Performing Songwriter*, January 23, 2016, http://performingsongwriter.com/girl-from-ipanema/

2 Pianta, "A Gênese da Bossa Nova."

Chapter 4

1 Paulo Mendes Campos, "Ser Brotinho," *O Cego de Ipanema* (Rio de Janeiro: Editora do Autor, 1960), 15.

2 Maria Ivanira Bastos, interview, Instituto Moreira Salles, 2013, https://www.youtube.com/watch?v=JfGEol_XfJI

3 Sérgio Porto, *As Cariocas* (Rio de Janeiro: Agir, 2006).

Chapter 6

1 Charles Perrone observes that de Moraes's original stage play sacrificed key elements of the myth. Perrone, "Don't Look Back: Myths, Conceptions and Receptions of Black Orpheus," *Studies in Latin American Popular Culture* XVII (1988): 155–77. David Treece argues that Marcel Camus's 1959 film was arguably closer to both the Greek myth and de Moraes's original conception. Treece, *Brazilian Jive: From Samba to Bossa and Rap* (London: Reaktion, 2013), 170. See also Charles Perrone, "Myth, Melopeia and Mimesis: Black Orpheus, Orfeu and Internationalization in Brazilian Popular Music," in *Brazilian Popular Music and Globalization*, eds. Charles Perrone and Christopher Dunn (Gainesville: University of Florida Press, 2001).

Chapter 8

1   Rubem Braga, *Ai de ti, Copacabana* (Rio de Janeiro: Editora do Autor, 1960).

Chapter 9

1   Whitney Balliett, *Collected Works: A Journal of Jazz* (New York: St. Martins), 184.

2   Castro, "Anatomia de um disco."

3   For full biographical coverage of Stan Getz, see Donald Maggin, *Stan Getz: A Life in Jazz* (New York: Harper Perennial, 1997); and Dave Gelly, *Stan Getz: Nobody Else but Me* (San Francisco: Backbeat, 2002).

Chapter 10

1   Vinicius de Moraes, *Orfeu da Conceição* (São Paulo: Companhia das Letras, 2013), 10.

Chapter 11

1 *Cancioneiro Jobim: Obras Completas, vol. 2, 1959–1965*
(Rio de Janeiro: Jobim Music, 2004); For careful analysis of
harmony in bossa nova, see José Estevam Gava, *A linguagem
harmonica da bossa nova* (São Paulo: Editora Unesp, 2002).

Chapter 17

1 Gene Lees, "Bossa Nova: Anatomy of a Travesty," *Downbeat*,
February 14, 1963, 22–24. For further analysis of jazz criticism
of bossa nova in the United States, see Christopher Dunn,
"Bossa Nova, the Aesthetics of Cool, and Jazz Criticism in
the Early 1960s," forthcoming. The article is also published
in Portuguese as "Por entre mascaras cool, twists mornos
e jazz fervente: a bossa nova no cenário norte-americano,"
in Garcia, *João Gilberto*, 251–69. For analysis of the brief
bossa nova dance fad in the United States, see Kariann
Goldschmitt, "Bossa Mundo: Brazilian Popular Music's Global
Transformations, 1938-2008," PhD dissertation, Musicology,
UCLA, 2009, 71–117.

Chapter 18

1 David Treece analyzes the tension between Jobim's modal
melodies and chromatic harmonies in *Brazilian Jive: From
Samba to Bossa and Rap*. See his discussion of "A Garota de
Ipanema" and "Águas de Março" in particular, pp. 101–5 and
109–11.

Chapter 19

1   Treece, *Brazilian Jive*, 98

Chapter 20

1   Abigail McEwen, "Olga Albizu and the Borders of Abstraction," *American Art* 29, no. 2 (2015): 103.

2   Michael Jarrett, *Pressed for All Time: Producing the Great Jazz Albums from Louis Armstrong and Billie Holiday to Miles Davis and Diana Krall* (Chapel Hill: University of North Carolina Press, 2016), 98.

3   McEwen, "Olga Albizu and the Borders of Abstraction," 101.

Chapter 24

1   Creed Taylor interviewed in Jarrett, *Pressed for All Time,* 98.

2   For an extensive but by no means exhaustive list of uses of movies and television shows that use "The Girl from Ipanema" in elevator scenes, see Joe Scaramanga, "Movies that Use the Girl from Ipanema in Lift Scenes." One amusing aspect of this blog post is that several reader comments suggest that, for many readers, "The Girl from Ipanema" is interchangeable with any other vaguely bossa nova background music played on synthesizer. https://letterboxd.com/joescaramanga/list/movies-that-use-the-girl-from-ipanema-in/

Index

Note: Page numbers followed by "f" indicate figures/photographs.

Index